the

TWILIGHT LANGUAGE

of

GORAKH BODH

Yogic Commentary

by

Shailendra Sharma

ISBN-10: 1548017736
ISBN-13: 978-1548017736

Introduction

These who accomplish the impossible,
Who [thunder] in the clear sky,
Who unlock [the state of] Unmuni,
These who reverse the breath say reverse things.

Gorakh Bani
"The Sayings of Gorakh"

Hatha Yoga Pradipika begins with: "Yoga was first known to Gorakhnath and Matsyendranath, and Swatmarama Yogi knew it by the grace of these two."

Gorakh Bodh ("Illumination of Gorakh") is an obscure ancient Hindi text by Nath Yogis, written as an intense dialog between Gorakhnath and his Teacher, Matsyendranath. Both of these two givers of the great knowledge of yoga are considered to be immortal.

Founder of Naths, Matsyendranatha or Machhendranath, left several sacred texts belonging to this mystical school. He is believed to be the author of *Kaulajnananirnaya* ("Deciding wisdom of Kaulas") and supposedly wrote *Yogavishaya* ("The Subject of Yoga") under the pen-name Minanath. There is no certainty of his dates; he supposedly lived between the eighth and tenth centuries.

His disciple, Gorakhanath, is widely known and respected in India as a great siddha. He wrote *Siddhasiddhantapaddhati* ("Siddha's conclusive Methods") and *Amaraughaprabodha* ("Knowing the Immortality"). His other work, *Amaraughashasana*, or

"Rules of Immortality," describes the methods of conquering time and death, a path to the states of non-duality and *amaraughasiddhi*, or the state of immortality.

Shiva followers, the Naths, regard Him as pure Consciousness, whereas Shakti, his energy, is the source of change and of the varied experiences related to it.

For the Nath yogis, the achievement of liberation in life is the main goal. Outer religious practices and scriptural knowledge are considered to be of a lesser value. Their only emphasis is on a direct way, as short as possible, a path through which a mystic discovers within himself an experience of the energy of the Universe.

The Naths believe in possibility of eternalizing human life by transcending the "lower" self (through control of mind and Prana – vital breath and life force energy) into the "upper" state of higher Consciousness.

Also called "Sahajiya," the Nathas are adepts of spontaneity, following simplicity of heart and mind.

At initial stages of yogic practice, the control of vital air is a crucial key for transendence of Self in Itself. Controlled breath and mind naturally infill the state of true spontaneity, *Sahaj*, finally merging into *Unmani* – the state of self-transcendence (when limited Self merges with the true "I"). Through *sahaj samadhi* thought becomes absorbed in bliss, the false sense of objectivity and duality weakens and ultimately disappears. This is achieved via Kumbhaka Mudra: breath is infused into the Sushumna channel through the unifying movement of inhalations and exhalations; thought becomes still, calming all senses.

The yogi recognizes the inner spontaneous sound (Anahat Naad) and keeps on listening to it, directing Prana into the median way. Kundalini awakens and rises to the highest center where She unites with Shiva. It is a natural ("sahaj") way of attaining Unmani (the state beyond thought), and that's how one becomes an *avadhut* ("avadhu" means "unattached" or, to be linguistically precise, "without a bride") and achieves liberation.

For such an ambitious task, an adept will need to find a true Guru who belongs to an *avadhu siddha* lineage and is revered as equal to Shiva himself. Such a Teacher can explain to his disciple the art of breath retention and the very process of absorption of mind with following awakening of Kundalini without any visible efforts from his own side.

Theoretical and practical knowledge given by the Guru suggests direct verbal transfer of Gyan. At a certain point of his sadhana (practice), the seeker starts to absorb the given teaching by the intuitive or above-intuitive approach; logical, discursive and ritual methods become secondary, as the persona of spiritual teacher carries utmost importance and meaning.

To keep their practices secret, the Naths used merely allusive language comprehended only by initiated adepts. The twilight, or "upside-down," language of *Gorakh Bodh* is also called "sandhya bhasha," an intentional manner of speech where allegoric narration forms a "double bottom," a layer of secret knowledge in seemingly plain content.

Written in ancient Hindi, the text of *Gorakh Bodh* appears obscure and dimmed. But even after decoding the puzzle of linguistics and yogic terms, the true meaning of the text will still remain a mystery for a non-initiated reader.

To find and meet an accomplished follower of the strict Nath discipline and a knowledgeable scholar of lineage texts is difficult. To comprehend the real sense of metaphoric riddles in this dialog between the ancient immortal yogis is an even more challenging task.

The text holds numerous references to the metaphysical cosmogony of Prana and Spirit, repeatedly stressing the importance of empirical knowledge. In plain words, self-realization can be achieved only through personal experience via persistent yogic practice of breath refinement, which develops a higher level of consciousness. Gradually merely physical aspects of the breath practice unfold its metaphysical core and goal.

Repetitiveness is part of Indian philosophic tradition: a guru transfers knowledge to his disciple by explaining different facets of one subject and by pointing at unexpected angles to expand mind. The poetic lines of archaic, grassroots level Hindi of *Gorakh Bodh* reflect this approach: meanings of the sound, breath, inner and outer voids and cognition of Time and timeless existence are questioned and explained in a series of seemingly repetitive fragments. Realization comes when the given Gyan is not only absorbed by the seeker mentally but, more importantly, when one lives through and by it.

The contemporary yogic commentary on the ancient text, "The Twilight Language of Gorakh Bodh," helps to understand the sublime and hidden methods of transference of knowledge. Detailed clarifications of terms and their deeper meanings are given in light of Babaji Kriya Yoga tradition. The author unveils hidden aspects of the ancient teaching rather than pursues the exactness of linguistic interpretation

However, we believe that both goals were achieved by Shri Shailendra Sharma, who gives profound and deep commentaries on the mysticism of higher yoga and its true goal.

Katia Mossin

Foreword by Shailendra Sharma

I hope that by reading this book people will realize that spirituality does not depend on any faith or religious devotion.

The true spirituality is a state of ever-wandering spirit, eager to question and receive essential knowledge and to move further. Even after crossing the threshold of immortality Gorakshanath continues to search for answers.

This intense dialog between a Guru and a disciple should be read by everyone who aspires to travel the path of yoga. Another work, comparable in the magnitude of direct knowledge communicated by a teacher to his disciple, is *Tripura Rahasya*, where Parashurama converses with Dattatreya.

Gorakh Bodh is a hard core practical discussion, far from philosophical disputes. It states what can be done and achieved because it had been done and had been achieved by the conversing yogis themselves.

The purpose of riddles and paradoxes presented in the text is to convey mystical knowledge only to the true seekers. The Naths have always been a secret order and full access to the teaching could be gained only after years of vigorous practice under the guidance (and with the blessing) of a true Guru.

While recording these commentaries, I was asked about the repetitiveness of the questions: why does Gorakshanath, already an immortal yogi, continue to place seemingly similar inquiries?

This text was left for us, the descendants, out of mercy and by the grace of these great teachers, who knew that children learn best through repetitions. By reaching immortality, these great adepts had obtained a luxury of unlimited time to examine every step of the path which took them there.

Some of the shlokas are left without comments: words of the masters carry a direct message to experienced yogis who will grasp its sense without additional explanation.

Every Hindi word in the text of *Gorakh Bodh* gives a certain flavor to every particular question and answer, enriching and deepening their meaning. The twilight language itself is a powerful and valuable "commodity" alluding to the secrets of immortality and divine life. Immortal beings are considered to be capable of creating future for themselves and may partake the future of some mortals, imbedding it in the ornament of their own fate. May this book become an inspiration for those who truly believe in the possibility of shaping an extraordinary future for themselves.

The very meaning of immortality could be summed up as follows:

Transformation of the future into past is Life.
Absolute transformation of the future into past is Death.
Unlimited future is immortality...

Shailendra Sharma

गोरख बोध

GORAKH BODH

────────────────── 1 ──────────────────

गोरख उवाच

स्वामीजी तुम गुरु गोसाईं,
अम्हेज शिष शब्द एक बूझिबा
दया करि कहबा, मन कुनि करि बाशेंस?
आरंभ चेला कैसे करि रहै?
सतगुरु होय सो पूछ्यां कहे ॥

Gorakh says:

Swami ji! You are the respected Guru.
Being only a disciple, I'd like to ask.
Have mercy, kindly tell:
How can mind be taken under control?
How should a beginner disciple live and what
should he do?
You are the true Guru, kindly answer my question.

ᶜᵔ᷉ The psychomental apparatus and limited empirical consciousness of each living being is formed by three elements – Manas, Buddhi and Ahamkar. Together with the five gross elements (panchamahabhuta), they belong to the eight elements of Prakriti. Manas (mind) creates concepts and ideas, Buddhi (intellect) gives intuitive knowledge, Ahamkar (ego, or literally, "I act") gives a sense of self, limited by mind, body and senses.

In this dialog the Naths refer to an advanced yogic intellect, which develops as a result of practice of pranayamas and signifies the Mind in Its totality.

13

When immortality of the body has been achieved, such a mind obtains its real depth and is no longer affected by external impressions. Only he who has managed to reach immortality while residing in the body is capable of contemplation on the consciousness of Time and Void. It is a luxury enjoyed by the selected few.

By the time these instructions were given, both participants of this famous dialog – Guru Matsyendranath and his disciple Gorakhnath – had reached this state. The conversation takes place when Gorakhnath has just stepped into eternity by attaining an imperishable "diamond body."

At the beginning of a new phase he prepares to move even beyond the limits of physical immortality, being directed by his Guru.

-- 2 --

श्री मच्छन्द्र उवाच

अवधू रहबा तो हांदां बाटाँ, रुख वृक्ष की छाया ।
तजि बातों काम क्रोध लोभ मोह संसार की माया ॥
आप सूँ गोष्ठि अनन्त विचार निंद्रा अल्प अहार ।
आरंभ चेला ऐसे रहै, गोरख सुणो मच्छन्द्र कहै ॥

Shri Machhendra says:

If you [want to] live as unattached (*avadhu*), then
Wander and rest in a shadow of a dry tree,
Leave desire, anger, greed, lust, illusions of the
world.
Listen and converse with yourself,
Contemplate upon Infinity (*anant*), sleep and
eat little.
This way a beginner disciple should live.
Listen, Gorakh, thus says Machhendra.

꩜ Recommendation to live without any earthly attachment is given by one immortal being to another. Listening to this teaching, one can wonder if even *Bhagavad Gita* itself was written as a manual for immortals because of complexity of the path to enlightenment...

The message is: "Don't cling to your house, leave everything, remain unattached and continue to move on."

Even the name by which Guru continuously addresses Gorakhnath carries a clear reference to the nature of his fate: "avadhu" means "one without a bride," "unattached."

Renunciation of all earthly attachments is not exactly a personal decision or a result of conscious effort: it is a conditioned state of mind, which appears as an outcome of mental, physical and spiritual practice. Such renunciation can be called an achievement.

Listen and converse with yourself, contemplate upon Infinity (anant)

When your spirit becomes a guru and your mind becomes a disciple – only then conversing with yourself will be possible.

Accepting your own spirit as a Teacher will grant enlightenment, leading to the supernatural realm of "afterlife," into the Endless state.

3

गोरख उवाच

स्वामीजी! कोण देखना कोण विचारना,
कोण तत्त ले धरिवा सार।
कोण देश मस्तक मुंडाईया,
कौण ज्ञान ले उतरवा पार॥

Gorakh says:

Swami ji! What should one see?
What should one think of?
With the help of which elements
should one realize the essence?
By whose order should one have his head shaved?
Armed with which knowledge should one cross
Beyond to the other side [of Samsara's ocean]?

---- 4 ----

श्री मच्छन्द्र उवाच

अवधू आपा देखिबा, अनंत विचारवा,
तत्त ले धरिवा सार।
गुरु का शब्द ले मस्तक मुंडाइबा,
ब्रह्म ज्ञान ले उतरबा पार॥

Shri Machhendra says:

Avadhu, see your own Self, contemplate upon
Infinity (*anant*).
Cognize the essence with the help of reality (*tattva*).
Have your head shaved as per word of Guru.
With the help of Brahma-knowledge
(*brahma gyan*) cross beyond to the other side.

ᑯᗐ The guidance is given to a highly accomplished yogi, who already went through an experience of over a thousand samadhis.

See your own Self, contemplate upon Infinity (anant)

Anant is often defined as "Endless Time." This shloka instructs the adept to contemplate on Time.

Cognize the essence with the help of reality (tattva)

Here "reality" means *tattva* – the original elements and the essence of all things, the essence of Time.

By contemplating on tattva of Time, a yogi becomes aware of

19

every process in the creation: he perceives every single thing existing in the universe and simultaneously observes every movement and action. This is a state of extreme awareness, or Samadhi.

Have your head shaved as per word of Guru

"Sanchit karma," or the memory of all previously "committed" karmic deeds, is in our DNA memory. Technically, hair is a carrier of most of the *sanskaras* – mental imprints of the past.

When a newly initiated *chela* (disciple) shaves off his hair by the word of his Guru, it is believed that all old karmic DNA traces – imprints and deep memories, associated with the past – are erased and new information (teaching) can be absorbed and processed.

Gorakh Bodh describes this process with precision: By Guru's word ("shabd"), all previous perceptions and habits associated with them, all influences of old instincts and unrealized desires are cut away, all ties with the past are erased.

Firmly installed in the practice, the yogi will become mature enough not to be troubled by old memories and to extract wisdom from past experiences.

With the help of Brahma-knowledge (brahma gyan) cross beyond to the other side

The expression "Samsar sagar," or "the ocean of Samsara," is commonly known in India.

Gorakhnath had just stepped into physical immortality by gaining an indestructible diamond body. But he is still present in the physical body and will continue to exist in the gross world. It is Guru's duty to remind Gorakhnath that he is still living in Samsara and needs to cross this ocean.

The path to the knowledge is given by Brahma Gyan.*

---

* Brahma Gyan, or Atma Gyan ("Self-Knowledge"), is the knowledge of the real self.

Soul travels from comprehension of its creation to the state beyond creation – Parabrahman, beyond duality, birth and death; eternal and indestructible, it realizes the Creator and His Creation.

5

गोरख उवाच

स्वामीजी, मन का कौण रूप,
पवन का कौण आकार।
दम की कौण दशा,
साधिबा कौण द्वार॥

Gorakh says:

Swami ji, what is the form of mind?
What is the form of breath?
What is the state of vital breath?
Toward which door [of the body] should one
direct [yogic] practice?

6

श्री मच्छन्द्र उवाच

अवधू, मन का शुन्य रूप,
पवन का निरालंब आकार ।
दम की अलेख दशा,
साधिबा दसवें द्वार ॥

Shri Machhendra says:

Avadhu, void (*shunya*) is the form of mind.
Breath (*pavan*) has no form, no shelter.
Vital breath (*dam*) has indescribable,
                              invisible states.
Practice [the method of] the tenth door.

∽ This shloka starts the sequence of questions and answers on the nature of breath and its origin.

To understand the origin of life force, or Prana, one should look no farther than *Shiva Sutras*; the following exposition illustrates the unseparable cosmogony of Time, Void and Prana:

Naisargikah pranasambandhah [43]
There is a natural connection with Prana (Shiva).

Shiva, the creator and supporter of the universe, destroys it when its cycle comes to an end.

Being Prana of all Pranas of this Creation, Shiva Mahakala, or the great Time, manifests in the human body in the form of Prana.

All embodied things and processes of this world are naturally connected with Shiva-Prana; He exists everywhere yet seems to be non-existent and perceived as Time.

Although we constantly feel Its flow, Time remains beyond all sensations and limits of our experience. Only those whose consciousness is fully developed by understanding the essence of Time may unite with It. Breath of Life in all beings, Prana is naturally linked to the Supreme Tattva – Time.

Time manifests Prana, and Prana returns back to the Time, dissolving in It.

Out of the greatness of Time, Conscious Void evinces Itself in the form of energy (Shakti), and Its creative force supports all things in this universe.

Perceptible by the senses, Conscious Matter, or body of this creation, is born out of union of Time and Void.

Everlasting and unchanged, life-giving, creative and fertile Shakti of this material world – Emptiness – is the basis of all movements and actions, occurring in It.

Emptiness pervades Time; being the root consciousness of conscious Emptiness, Time Itself pervades the Void.

Great Time Itself is the Prana, or the vital force, of Void and Matter; permeating all existing creation, it always remains transcendent.

Void (shunya) is the form of mind

The Hindi term for "void" – "shunya" – literally translates as "emptiness" as well as "zero." Self-void represented by Kutastha appears in the practice of Yoni Mudra. It is a point of self-zero, or self-Shunya, mastered by the practitioner. It is also said that the appearance of a dark circle with a golden aura around it signals a temporary movement of Kundalini on the verge of awakening.

Guru Matsyendranath defines the nature of mind, pointing at the Void as its root and form.

Universal Shunya is the basis of all existing Matter, as 99.9% of the surrounding material world consists of emptiness, including human bodies: they are nothing but concentrated expressions of Void.

Being the source of its own origin, Void precedes mind.

Great Emptiness is absolutely conscious: only a conscious entity can give birth to another consciousness.

Together with jiva, the individual soul, Void infills every cell of the body and every particle of the material world surrounding it.

Individual mind confirms the fact of existence to its carrier; only acute consciousness can register the very fact of existence ("I am").

Condensed Consciousness expresses Itself in the form of individual physical bodies, while physical brain serves as the seat of mind, its hardware.

In the fourth chapter of *Hatha Yoga Pradipika* Swatmarama describes inner and outer voids. The exploration and realization of those voids takes the seeker "beyond mind" – a yogi is lead to the Unmuni state by the sound of the Void.

When all granthis are cleared, the yogi's mind merges with the outer Void as he listens to the greatness of eternal Naad in the state of Samadhi.

Awareness of the sound allows the seeker's conscious mind to enter the realm of subconsciousness.

This step signifies the beginning of comprehension of the Void's Consciousness.

Once the yogi has established himself in the Void, he will discover its greatest property, Consciousness, also called the Universal Mind, for lack of better terms.

Shall we consider nature to be different from its forms or separate the form from its nature?

Nature is expressed in a vast variety and each form has its own nature. They complement and offset each other.

The true nature of mind reflects greater Void Itself and that's why Shunya, or Emptiness, is greatly stressed upon in Yoga.

Vital breath (dam) has indescribable, invisible states

Formless and invisible, breath has never been seen. Out of five elements, Vayu (air) and Akash (ether) also remain unseen; always bound together, they form a brotherhood.

Akash, or the sky, is visible but cannot be touched; even its color is nothing but an optical illusion.

Formless ether is still "grosser" in comparison with the Void: Emptiness itself is more "formless" than the substance which infills it.

The powerful source of life, vital breath animates every carrier and is considered to be a true Shakti, or force which grants power and protection.

Part of Vayu's properties and "responsibilities" is to express Life Itself. Closely connected with Earth, the air element Vayu acts as Its protector. Being connected with the earth element in the human body, Vayu animates and protects our earthly bodies as vital breath. Vital breath is a carrier of Prana, which is even more subtle than Vayu.

The practitioner becomes aware of the formless and invisible ether element Akash by contemplating upon it; but first he studies and understands the nature of Vayu, or vital breath, through steady performance of pranayamas.

Breath practice removes ignorance and intellectual limitations. Such "cleansing" results in the emergence of a super-intellect, able to analyze and absorb the deepest knowledge.

At that stage the yogi has already explored and realized subtle elements – he leaves them behind and moves beyond Akash, becoming aware of the Void.

Understanding and realization of the Void is possible only with sequential steps on this path: by understanding the nature of breath, by purification and "cleansing" by and through it, by befriending it and taking its guidance on the path to the higher realms.

"Through the miraculous pill of the breath
You are dwelling in Akash
Inside yourself is a sky and Kailash
The dhobi (laundress) from the underworld climbs up in the
emptiness"

Gorakh Bani

Practice [the method of] the tenth door

"At the tenth door the avadhut has undone the lock," says Gorakhnath in one of his treatises.

What is referred to as "the method of the tenth door" is the Tenth door of Brahma.

Human body is compared to a temple with nine doors, but the power of yogic tapas (vigorous practice) develops the tenth gate, commonly known as Brahmarandhra. He who is able to open this door during his lifetime gains control over all nadis (energy channels) of his body.

To leave one's body through the tenth door of Brahma is a privilege for only a few highly advanced sadhaks (adepts). Initiated by direct instructions from the Guru or God Himself, such a journey requires a life-long time of dedicated preparation. Adepts transfer their full fate in the discipline they follow and into the teaching of the Guru. At the time of physical death, the yogi will open this door from inside to let the spirit exit the used and worn shell of the body.

Entry into Sushumna Nadi lies at the tail of the sleeping snake, in Muladhara: this orifice is called Brahmadvaar; let's agree that this is the threshold of the door of Brahma. In order to enter the middle channel, one has to start pulling the door handle, so to speak.

When Kundalini has risen by the union of Prana and Apana, which entered Sushumna through Brahmadvaar, the "serpent energy" travels up through the length of the spine to the top of the skull. There it arrives at the mouth of Shankhini – another opening of the door of Brahma which releases the current of energy. Such is a journey – from Brahmadvaar at Muladhara center to Brahmarandhra, the chamber of Brahma.

The entire Sushumna itself is the gate of Brahma. Opening the door of Sushumna in Muladhara is the act of opening the tenth door.

गोरख उवाच

स्वामीजी, कोण पेड़ बिन डाल,
कौण पंख बिन सूआ।
कोण पाल बिन नार,
कौण बिन कोल मूआ॥

Gorakh says:

Swami ji, what is a tree without a branch?
What is a parrot without wings?
What is a tent without a rope?
What is death without dying?

--- **8** ---

श्री मच्छन्द्र उवाच

अवधू, पवन पेड़ बिन डाल,
मन पंख बिन सूआ ।
धीरज पाल बिन नार,
निद्रा बिन काल मूआ ॥

Shri Machhendra says:

Avadhu, breath (*pavan*) is a tree without a branch.
Mind is a parrot without wings.
Patience (*dhiraj*) is a tent without a rope.
Sleep is death without dying.

∾ The metaphoric riddles of yogic language pass on great knowledge.

Breath (pavan) is a tree without a branch.
Mind is a parrot without wings

Every breathing creature on this planet has the same experience at the moment of birth: vital Prana, or power of Life, enters the heart and triggers the mechanism of drawing air into the body by means of breath.

Prana will remain in the body till the very end of life; then Apana will switch off the breathing mechanism, cutting air supply, and Prana will move out, leaving the used equipment behind.

The fuel of life and the carrier of vital force, breath is a thread by which Prana holds life inside the body, being itself, in turn, held captive by Apana.

Breath supports the tree of life with all its strength but without a visible branch or trunk.

There is another description of breath's force and its importance: "I saw a wall made only of sand and a pillar of Vayu and I am amazed: how is it standing...?"

Body is aptly compared to sand, supported only by vital breath, the pillar of Vayu.

Why specifically the parrot is named here and not any other bird? Because not every bird talks in the human language: a wingless talking parrot cannot fly away from its cage just as the ever chatting mind trapped inside the skull.

"Dhiraj" signifies great yogic self-control and patience that can hold the tent of mind.

Vital breath, mind and sleep – these various conditions and states of existence are interconnected. Life Itself combines together Its own different forms and expressions.

Sleep, also known as "little death," revives mind nightly; death revives it as well by transferring consciousness to another state, into another form of existence in the astral plane.

Unaware of the body, people enter the dreamland every night, visiting another side of life.

Reviving and revitalizing itself, mind is on the loose in the astral realm, while brain is managing the sleeping body.

In the morning mind will return to the body. Life will enter another vessel of Atma with a new birth, death will open yet another door for a new journey of ever wandering spirit.

33

9

गोरख उवाच

स्वामीजी! कौण बीरज कौण खेत,
कौण श्रवण कौण नैत ।
कौण जोग कौण जुक्ति,
कौण मोक्ष कौण मुक्ति ॥

Gorakh says:

Swami ji! What is a seed? What is a field?
What is hearing? What is seeing?
What is yoga? What is the
                        method [of practicing it]?
What is liberation? What is salvation?

10

श्री मच्छन्द्र उवाच

अवधू! मंत्र बीरज मति क्षेत्र,
सुरति श्रवण निरती नैत्र।
करम जोग धूरम जुगति,
ज्योति मोक्ष बिज्वाला मुक्ति॥

Shri Machhendra says:

Avadhu! Mantra is a seed;
[Perceptive] intellect is a field.
[Attentive] consciousness (*surati*) is hearing;
Immersion (*nirati*) is seeing.
Action is yoga; dharma is the method.
Light is liberation; refulgence is salvation.

Mantra is a seed

〜 The true meaning of the term "mantra" goes far beyond the religious chants of "Hare Krishna" or "Om Namah Shivaya": the literal translation of "mantra" is "very mysterious secret," or "gupta rahasya."

During initiation into Kriya Yoga the disciple receives a secret teaching and it becomes a mantra, seed ("bija") of mystery planted into the seeker.

The seed of the great secret grows in the womb of perceptive mind, triggering the development of higher consciousness.

[Perceptive] intellect is a field

Ability of the differentiating mind (or intellect) to perceive a mantra forms the womb, the carrier of the seed. It can also be compared to the field where a planted seed hibernates before emerging to the surface from the soil.

In the womb of perception the seed of the secret knowledge will evolve and grow, just like a fetus develops for birth.

When the embryo of consciousness has grown in the womb of perception, its deliverance will result in the state of nirvana.

[Attentive] consciousness (surati) is hearing

The air element, or Vayu, is recognized by *sparsh*, or tactile sense, and experienced via inhalation through the nose, mouth and lungs.

The subtle element of ether, or the sky, Akash is perceived with the help of another tanmatra – Shabd, or sound. That's why *Gorakh Bodh* stresses the importance of attentive and conscious perception that is able to register sound as a direct property of the Void.

The subtlest of all senses, hearing is the direct recipient of Shabd, message from the Void.

Myriads of subtle cosmic and earth sounds simply can't be registered by ordinary limited hearing tools.

"Vibration" is a sub-root of the word "shabd": if a yogi develops the ability to "catch" the vibration of the Void's cosmic sound with the help of direct hearing (attention of mind), then he will be able to get to its primordial source. Such is the definition of true hearing.

The ability to comprehend the subtlety of vibration allows one to travel to the source of the sound and grants entry to the realm which lies beyond Akash and the five elements. This dimension can be reached by a selected few.

Empowered by the knowledge of the secret teaching of mantra and by its practice, the yogi will connect with the Consciousness of Void. It will introduce him to the Consciousness of Time, which holds the essence of all Creation in Itself.

When one has arrived at that point, where else can he travel from there? There will be no need to explore other realms of the so-called hells or heavens: the yogi will be able to experience all of it with a new level of super-consciousness.

The five elements of Creation are not the essence of the Creation, they are just construction materials – the bricks and mortar that this Creation is made of.

One example might give us an idea about the essence of things: this house is made of bricks but what is the essence of this house?

By examining this house brick by brick we will never discover the essence. The initial shape of the structure and the creative energy, Shakti, came together to play in the builder's mind; it is where the future form of the building took its shape first. The seed essence of this house is in the consciousness of the architect who planned it. It was expressed in the material form and we are now sitting inside it.

The essence of the house existed long before the architect expressed it in the drawings and it was built with stone and mortar. The essence of the form was simply discovered by applying imagination to the very idea of the form – and shape emerged from the depth of inquiring mind.

Bricks don't carry the essence of the house; the essence of a human body is not in the tissue of its flesh. It lies somewhere else, in the initial consciousness manifested through the body.

Once established in himself through realization of the highest consciousness, the yogi will grasp his own essence, and there will be no need to search any further.

The famous Krishna devotee Mira Bai, who lived five centuries ago, gave a perfect answer to someone who asked her why she remained in one place after having roamed around for a long time: "My lover is inside me – I don't need to go anywhere."

Immersion (nirati) is seeing

Physical vision allows us to receive information only about 60% of the material world, and even this so-called visible reality is merely a reflection of light from the exposed surfaces, formed by the gross elements. Therefore, eye vision can't be considered complete and reliable, as it catches only reflections of light which come from different objects, without seeing these objects in full.

Lucifer (or "Light bringer") was proclaimed a "Devil" because of a simple act of bringing the light (i.e. differentiating knowledge) to people, which created a great confusion in their minds.

The humanity saw just a reflection of truth and started to take it as the Ultimate Reality. But the true essence of Reality can't be seen through "naked eyes," it can only be perceived by mind. Light rays bounce from the frontal surfaces of objects, creating only 60% of visually perceptible reflections. Some facets are never "shined upon" by light, and partially visible reality forms an incomplete picture.

The entire material world consists of endless combinations of five elements, but only three gross elements (earth, water and fire) are able to reflect light. Therefore, eyes are able to capture and perceive only these three elements – or, rather, partial reflection of light from these elements.

Yes, physical vision is not perfect, and only discriminating mind allows full "vision."

Distinction of different objects and concepts (including the contrast of good and bad) is just the beginning of superficial differentiation.

Starting with basic superficial differentiation, one will arrive at discrimination between the essence of life and creation; the seeker will start to recognize it everywhere.

We should remember that all things, events and notions, good and bad, are carriers of the essence of creation contained within them.

Yoga Sutras describe Dharana, Dhyan and Samadhi as the highest forms of immersion and submersion. Perception beyond the visible form is submersion into the true nature of the object.

But basic vision is always employed before this, as you have to take a good look at the object (or subject) to be able to contemplate upon its qualities. Another term for this process is Dharana.

Action is yoga; dharma is the method

The previous English translation* of another Hindi variant of

---

* Dr. Mohan Singh's "Gorakhnath and Medieval Hindu Mysticism." For more information, see "Sources and References" on page 311.

this line was given as: *"The ocean (uram) is joga and the earth (dhuram) is the method,"** and its poetic interpretation also carries a true statement.

Earth represents the body, an instrument of karma. Without the earth element, body will not be formed – who would be able to act, to practice yoga then?

The earthly body follows dharma, or the method of practicing the yoga of life.

Yoga (Joga) is a subject so vast and deep that ancient sages compared its art to an ocean. The adept will continue to swim in its waters and may cross it with the help of advanced skills.

Yoga of action, or karma yoga, might be translated directly as kriya yoga: understanding of the right methods of following the true Dharma will develop only with consistency of kriya yoga practice.

Light is liberation

When the seeker develops inner understanding, it is compared with light ("jyoti"): *"... and the light of understanding dawned on him."*

Gorakh Bodh and other yogic texts define the discovery of such understanding as a path to liberation.

Recognition of one's own Self happens in the course of yogic practice: during Yoni Mudra the practitioner sees Kutastha, its dark circle has a brightly lighted aura; the golden ring of Shiva (Prana) embraces the dark core of Shakti (Apana).

---

* उंरम जोग धुरम जुगति

In Sanskrit "kutastha" means "immortal spirit": it is your own Atma and your immortal substance; it illuminates the path to self-discovery and liberation from the darkness of ignorance. Purely physical processes of practice will culminate in metaphysical experiences.

The bright light of Kutastha in Yoni Mudra is a direct result of Khechari Mudra performed with a retained breath.

Occasional absence of Kutastha during practice does not necessarily indicate that the infusion of Prana and Apana into the median channel failed: their union simply needs privacy, so to speak, and the practitioner should continue to "build a relationship of trust" with his own breath.

Refulgence is salvation

Yogic practice carries the fiery seed of knowledge, which will burn old limitations and ignite the mind, revealing the essence of Creation.

Understanding of this essence will come as a salvation for the mind, liberating it from constraints.

A small sparkle, a seed of light of realization can trigger a volcanic fire, an eruption of pure consciousness. Liberation comes when the seeker realizes the source of his own creation and the very reason he was created for: it ignites the powerful fire of revelation or understanding of the whole creation. Such is the process – from a speckle of light to the eruption of volcanic fire, from liberation to salvation.

The light of liberation does not signify total destruction, as the metaphor itself conveys an absolutely different meaning.

The very idea of sudden forceful destruction and burning of karmas, sins, bad thoughts and deeds is an impact of religious concepts on our mind. Yogis simply call all this ballast *klesha*, "progress-hinderers" – they are no more than that. Persistence of yogic practice can burn down kleshas; in the end, when all unnecessary things become ashes, the essence of Creation will be revealed.

And that's how discrimination comes. For the sake of observance of non-violence, such words as "destruction" or even "erasing the ignorance" should not be used at all. Any forceful attempt to destroy ignorance is an act of real violence. Ignorance should be studied instead, and this study will grant wider knowledge.

Guru Gorakhnath

11

गोरख उवाच

स्वामीजी! कौण मूल कौण बेला,
कौण गुरु कौण चेला।
कौण खैल कोण मेला,
कौण तत ले रमे अकेला॥

Gorakh says:

Swami ji! What is a root; what is a creeper?
Who is a teacher (*guru*); who is a disciple?
What is a field; what is a meeting (*mela*)?
With which essence (*tat*) should one
Enjoy solitude [self-contemplation]?

12

श्री मच्छन्द्र उवाच

अवधू! मन मूल पवन बेला,
शब्द गुरु सुरती चेला।
त्रिकुटि क्षैत्र उलटि मेला,
निरवाण तत ले रमो अकेला॥

Shri Machhendra says:

Avadhu! Mind is a root; breath is a creeper.
Word (*shabd*) is a teacher (*guru*),
Mind (*surati*) is a disciple.
[Above] the bridge of nose (*trikuti*) is the field
Where a meeting (*mela*) [takes place]
by reversing (*ulti*).
Based upon the truth of cessation [of physical
existence] (*nirvaan*),
One should enjoy solitude.

∾ This idea will be repeated continuously throughout the entire dialogue: to understand the nature of breath is to understand mind itself; control over one's breath takes the practitioner to the very source of consciousness; the creeper of breath entwines the root of mind.

Ida, Pingala and Sushumna come together in Trikuti: their meeting place lies above the bridge of nose between the eyebrows (Bhrumadhya).

YOGIC COMMENTARY by SHAILENDRA SHARMA

In this field an extraordinary meeting ("mela") takes place: jiva meets Ishvara.

When the flow of breath is reversed and turned back to its source, Ishvara, or Param Shiva, dwelling in mind, meets jiva. That's how a great meeting takes place.

The erected tongue in Khechari Mudra is drawn behind the upper soft palate, attaching itself (sticking) to the walls of the inner throat in 3 points: at the side of its tip, in the middle and then at the base; this is another form of Trikuti. A higher state of consciousness will be experienced in Trikuti only when the three points indicated above are stimulated properly.

Word (shabd) is a teacher (guru),
Mind (surati) is a disciple

The sound of Anahat Naad comes as the Primordial Word of the Supreme Guru, Time. It is the Word (Shabd) which is the source of existence of every jiva, or spirit: everything in this material world is generated by the initial vibration of the Sound, or by the word of Time.

A spirit arrives to the physical body from an unseen plane, a different dimension. Together with the pranic life force infused into a new carrier (the body), jiva remains there for a limited time.

During one's lifetime, an inquiring mind can make an attempt to connect with the spirit via the practice of breath control.

Then the spirit can reveal its deepest secrets: it will open up the vault of subconscious mind, where it had stored the vast memories of previous mysterious experiences collected during past journeys. Becoming a guru, the spirit guides the mind; and after a prolonged yogic practice the mind will no longer remain a disciple, it will merge with the spirit, becoming its guru, and will cross the boundaries of duality.

Conscious and Subconscious will unite as the Supreme Mind.

13

गोरख उवाच

स्वामीजी! कोण घर चंद कोण घर सूर,
कोण घर काल बजावे तूर।
कोण घर पांच तत्व सम रहे
सतगुरु होय सो बूझ्यां कहै॥

Gorakh says:

Swami ji! In which house is the moon;
In which house is the sun?
In what house does Time play the flute?
In which house do five elements pervade equally?
You are the true Guru, kindly explain.

--- **14** ---

श्री मच्छन्द्र उवाच

अवधू, मन घर चंद पवन घर सूर,
शुन घर काल बजावे तूर।
ज्ञान घर पांचों तत सम रहे,
ऐसा विचार मच्छन्द्र कहे॥

Shri Machhendra says:

Avadhu! Mind is the house of the moon;
Breath is the house of the sun.
Time plays the flute (*tur*) in the house of Void.
In the house of knowledge five elements
reside in equipoise (*sam rahe*).
Thus opinion utters Machhendra.

Mind is the house of the moon

～ Two immortals are discussing and esteeming different aspects and properties of a "moon" throughout the dialog.

In the cryptic language of yogis, "moon" stands for Prana, consciousness and immortality, being one of Shiva's names as well.

Western readers might benefit from understanding the roots of this concept and parallels by closely examining the OM symbol.

Crescent moon with a dot above it in this famous Sanskrit symbol is the seed (bija) mantra of Shiva, who represents eternity and everlasting life.

Another indicative name of the sound Om – endless vibration of Naad – is "pranava," derived from the word "prana."

The energy of the sun provides for the process of creation, the moon sustains and nurtures; the fire element, which prevails in all elements, has destructive powers.

Moon-Prana is the basis of mind or, rather, Prana is mind.

The giver of the birth of consciousness, Moon-Prana houses jiva, or the soul.

Mind contains part of the universal essence: it is both our consciousness and immortal spirit. We are alive because jiva inhibits our bodies, planted by the moon, the vital pranic force.

The English translation does not convey the common roots and connection of terms "spirit" and "life" properly.

In Hinduism such notions as "jiva" (meaning "spirit") and "jivan" (meaning "life") are imbedded into each other, forming an indivisible and integrated concept.

The importance of the key element in Kriya practice –Khechari Mudra – is so great that it is called "jivha." The term indicates the tongue, but its roots are in "jiva," the core of conscious existence. Khechari Mudra is the primary requirement and main condition for the practice of Kriya Yoga.

During the performance of this mudra, the yogi inserts his tongue into the cavity of the throat behind the upper soft palate. There, in the inner void, the outline of the tongue and the contour of the cavity form a silhouette of the crescent moon.

Yogis believe that successful performance of Khechari Mudra together with other techniques will result in super-consciousness.

But the very act of formation of the inner moon is impossible without jiva and its inquiring will.

In the absence of soul, the essence of Prana can never be understood or experienced.

Transcendence to higher consciousness, or "appearance of the moon," is an important yogic achievement. It allows to explore mind further by merging its two different states in the process of replacement of unconsciousness with consciousness and vice versa.

By reaching the state of supreme mind, the sadhak finally abandons duality.

Breath is the house of the sun

The intake of Prana animates the body; we sustain ourselves by burning this fuel of life. But excessive consumption of oxygen also speeds up aging process, incinerating the life essence. Breath carries dual powers: to animate and annihilate. Simultaneously with gifting body with life, it triggers the process of cindering its vitality.

Present in all five elements of creation, the fire of the sun strongly affects their primary qualities.

Extended everywhere, the fire element is the prevailing ingredient in all elements and the basis of their properties.

Condensed, Akash, or ether, is expressed as air. One of the main properties of air, inherited from Agni (fire), is the ability to dry and evaporate.

Concentrated and condensed air manifests itself as fire.

Condensed, fire becomes water; "cold fire," or combination of hydrogen and oxygen, is highly volatile and directly related to the power of Agni.

Condensed further, water turns into the earth element. Great fire lives in the core of the planet and exists in the nucleus of every atom structure.

Time plays the flute (tur) in the house of Void

An eternal tune played by the Time is the sound of Anahat Naad (also called Shabd, the universal Word). This shloka compares its resonance with the sound of Tura, long Rajasthani flute.

In the absence of instrument, music is still being played – it could be understood by going deeper into meditation (Dhyan) and becoming conscious of the Void.

Void is a musical instrument of Life; Its eternal sound (Anahat Naad) manifests countless notes as condensed combinations of five elements; it plays the melody of the Matter. Time plays in Void to create Life – and the very process of this creation is the music of Void.

The unique experience of the unobstructed Anahat Naad sound invites and guides the yogi to Void, allowing him to listen to the very melody of creation.

In the house of knowledge five elements reside in equipoise (sam rahe)

"Sam" defines a silent pause between notes, a momentary interval between musical sounds.

Enjoyment of music itself is an art of listening and capturing this moment of equilibrium of notes.

Five elements reside in the pause (in the "sam") of the sound of cosmic Naad: they are different notes born out of vibration. Everything in this world is vibratory by nature: when cosmic sounds are condensed in different ways, they transform into initial elements.

The Supreme Mind, Consciousness of the Void, or the house of knowledge, is where all elements rest in perfect harmony and balance. But the human body can also become a house of knowledge of deep mysteries of yoga.

The yogi achieves the balance of elements with the help of the cool nectar of immortality, Amrita. Enriched by Prana in the course of persistent sadhana,* it comes from "the moon" – consciousness.

Nectar's appearance is attributed to the calmness of controlled and tamed mind; physiologically, this substance is excreted by stimulated glands and certain brain centers.

The main objective of yogic practice is to direct the formed elixir to the heart, feeding Prana concentrated there, diverting it from falling into the fire of the digestive tract.

In the third and forth Kriya, special head movements stimulate the brain, which "floats" in the cerebral fluid. "Churning" of the brain results in the appearance of the "butter" of consciousness.

Directly connected with the Indian myth of churning the world ocean, Kriya Yoga first extracts all the poison accommodated by the ocean of the soul and then brings out the immortal nectar. All deepest metaphysics of the subtle

---

* Practice

processes are always supported by the physical body. It is used as a tool, as a vessel and precious carrier of the unique seed of consciousness recognized and awakened by yogic sadhana.

The elixir is "caught" by the practitioner via Khechari Mudra and directed into the heart, where it feeds concentrated Prana.

Amrita stays above and beyond the five elements, although carried by the liquid. In fact, being a catalytic agent, Amrita holds all the five elements together indefinitely.

Brought to the heart, Amrita supports the proper balance and quality of the five elements of the body.*

Enriched by the "nectar," now all-powerful Prana unites with Apana and enters Sushumna, gifting the yogi with the "changeless state," or eternal life.

---

* We will not comment on the nature of Ojas; its origin and properties were explained in full in various yogic texts.

However, it is worth mentioning that Ojas (collected in Hriday, the heart) and Amrita might start forming simultaneously.

15

गोरख उवाच

स्वामीजी, कोण अमावस कौण पड़वा,
कहां का महा रस कहां ले चढ़िबा।
कौण स्थान मन उनमुनि रहे,
सतगुरु होय सो पूछ्यां कहे॥

Gorakh says:

Swami ji! What is the new moon (*amaavas*);
What is the first day of a waxing crescent?
Which great elixir (*maha ras*) should be taken
and where to?
At what place does mind reside in the
state of self-transcendence?*
You are the true Guru, kindly answer the question.

---

* From Latin *transcendens* – "crossing over, superior, going beyond" –
in its broadest sense it is understood as a state beyond. In this translation
the term "self-transcendence" is used to indicate a departure
beyond self and ordinary mind into a state of thoughtlessness.

16

श्री मच्छन्द्र उवाच

अवधू! रवि अमावस चंद सू पड़वा,
अर्ध का महारस ऊर्ध ले चढ़िबा।
गगन स्थाने मन उनमुनि रहे,
ऐसा विचार मच्छन्द्र कहे॥

Shri Machhendra says:

Avadhu! Sun is [the cause of] the new moon
And the darkest night itself (*amaavas*).
Moon is the first day of a waxing crescent.
The great elixir of the middle (*ardh*) should be
taken upward (*urdh*).
In the space (*gagan*) [within us] mind resides
in self-transcendence (*unmuni*).
Thus opinion utters Machhendra.

∽ The life-giving element of the Sun resides in the fire of Apana. As long as Sun-Apana is active, Life will continue to manifest Itself, but it will bring the ignorance of mortality with it.

While Sun-Apana is active and holds Prana, we are trapped in the circle of Samsara, in the state of Amaavas. Existence in the darkness of ignorance of ordinary mortal life is called Amaavas.

A giver is also a taker: that's why the giver of the mortal life – Ravi – the Sun, or untamed Apana, should be treated as the darkest night.

As already explained in previous shlokas, the performance of Khechari Mudra stimulates the brain, which produces Amrita, or the nectar of life.

If not directed to the heart by certain yogic techniques, it eventually falls into the fire of digestive center.

Representing the intensive heat of the sun, Apana, or inner fire, devours and burns the elixir of eternal life, making death inevitable.

Only when the influence of Sun-Apana is over, and the new moon is manifested, the nectar of life flows uninterruptedly, allowing a possibility of achieving immortality.

New moon is a state of new consciousness, the symbol of everlasting life; the giver of Amrita, it brings light to the dark night of mortality.

The yogic treatise *Siddhasiddhantapaddhati* has an exact description of the process: "If the yogi meditates on Kaal,* nectar drips from the moon. Then, curling his tongue back in Khechari Mudra, he prevents this nectar from falling into the destructive fire of the navel region. Accordingly, he attains immortality."

But how could this metaphysical moon manifest its light?

As a Guru of Kriya Yoga, I can point out the one and only way of bringing light into inner darkness: with the practice of Yoni Mudra light will shine on your inner screen.

This great bright light of Kutastha in Yoni Mudra signifies the very essence of Prana as well as the presence of our own immortal spirit, or Atma.

---

* Time

The shining of Kutastha in Yoni Mudra manifests the rise of the new moon, or the new state of consciousness.

Merged with each other by breathlessness, Prana and Apana will enter the Sushumna; in Khechari Mudra Kutastha will rise and its light will manifest the eternity.

Installed as a Shiva lingam during Khechari Mudra, the tongue will receive the milk of immortality, and a true Abhishek of Shiva* will take place.

Which great elixir (maha ras) should be taken and where to? –
The great elixir of the middle (ardh) should be taken
upward (urdh)

Numerous philosophical discussions about the phenomenon of breath were conducted in the course of human history; still remaining a mystery, this very breath made these discussions possible.

Every aspiring yogi should try to understand the initial basics first. The seeker should try to develop higher sensitivity and awareness of the movement of Prana and Apana through the individual practice of breath control. It takes some time to understand their nature.

By offering Prana to Apana, yogis initiate the process of taking elixir of the middle ("ardh") to the upper ("urdh").

This exchange is the first step of the practice; then comes more refined and subtle awareness of conscious and subconscious mind. They will be brought into each other in the course of continuous consistent sadhana. It could be compared to the

---

* Ritual pouring of milk on a Shiva lingam.

work of an artist: first he outlines the silhouette of the painting with pencil and charcoal (Prana and Apana). Then he paints with the strokes of a paint brush, and mixed colors from the palette of consciousness and subconsciousness form a splendid masterpiece, the portrait of true Self.

For the sake of metaphoric comparison, let's draw some parallels between breath and a married couple, husband and wife, who live in the house of a body.

The husband brings enough money to support the household, but it is the woman who controls the spending and does the chores. After coming from work the husband rests, while the wife continues her chores. When Prana returns home, it rests; Apana continues to support and animate the body by distributing Prana's "earnings."

In the space (gagan) [within us] mind resides in self-transcendence (unmuni)

The word "gagan" allows several interpretations: Akash, heaven, space and Void, from where the sound comes. Like Akash, Mind resides in the Void – formless, untouched, unseen.

The actual word for "heaven" is "svarga" – with the root "sva," or "self," but it carries a very different meaning in proper translation.

"Svarga" is the heaven where the essence of self can be discovered.

Heaven discussed in this text can be reached when the seeker has established himself in himself by making conscious mind subconscious and subconscious mind conscious.

Eventually, such a yogi will cross the threshold of heaven and Time, led by that Mind.

But what is self-transcendence of mind if it is already limitless?

Body is an expression of the Consciousness, it represents the limiting idea of individual "self."

By moving beyond conscious ideas and impressions of self, one enters the state of self-transcendence.

98% of unexplored consciousness is called "subconscious"; it remains unknown to its carriers.

When the yogi enters the realm of subconscious and explores it, he discovers a new state called Unmuni.

Here "self" refers to the personal identity of "I," and the process describes the transcendence of the "portrait of self" that was created by limited conscious mind.

Transformation to a higher level will happen only when one submerges into the depth of unknown and unexplored subconsciousness.

It is the most important angle in this shloka: just submerge into yourself and claim your own heaven, find the kingdom of it.

गोरख उवाच

स्वामीजी, आदि का कौण गुरु,
धरती का कोण भरतार।
ज्ञान का कोण स्थान है,
शुन का कहाँ है द्वार॥

Gorakh says:

Swami ji! Who is the Guru of Origin;
Who is the spouse of the Earth?
What is the place of knowledge?
Where is the door to the Void?

—————————————— **18** ——————————————

श्री मच्छन्द्र उवाच

अवधू! आदि का अनादि गुरु,
धरती का अंबर भरतार।
ज्ञान का स्थान चिंतन है,
शुन का परचा द्वार॥

Shri Machhendra says:

Avadhu! The Eternal Beginningless (*anaadi*) is the
Guru of Origin.
Heaven (*ambar*) is the husband of the Earth.
[Continuous] pondering (*chintan*) is the
house of knowledge.
Knowing (*parcha*) is the door to the Void.

✿ Time is the eternal beginningless ("anaadi") Guru of
Creation; the first Teacher of all sages and rishis.

Time creates the body, impregnating it with the seed of
consciousness; mind develops in the womb of the physical shell;
being the First Guru, only Time grants true knowledge.

Being the cause of everything, It has no beginning or end.

Heaven (ambar) is the husband of the Earth

Ambar, Shunyata, Khali Akash – all these terms indicate
different aspects of Void.

Analyzed etymologically, "ambar" can reveal a direct connection with its "function." The Sanskrit word for "mother" is

"Amba"; "Ambar" is the "one to whom the mother belongs."

This statement is literally correct: mother Earth belongs to the Void, being married to the Great Emptiness.

The husband's duty is to protect his wife, and Vayu (Ambar, manifested as the Sky) wraps, shields and protects Earth (Vayu Mandal) from the brutality of cosmic impact.

Similar understanding of this great phenomenon and its basis could be traced in all ancient cultures and aboriginal beliefs.

According to the Greek mythology, Gaya was the great mother of the entire Universe; she was the giver of birth to Earth, and her union with Uranus, the "Sky," produced many gods...

Knowing* (parcha) is the door to the Void

Shabd (word-sound) invites the mind into the depths of subconsciousness; listening to the sound of Naad opens the door to realization. This realization is the recognition of the Void's consciousness.

To travel that far is nearly a miracle; on arrival the yogi reaches an absolutely new level of wisdom and understanding.

Awareness of the sound opens access to the Emptiness, or Shakti Itself: It might grant permission to enter It through the door of awareness of Naad.

---

* "Knowing" was first translated as "realization" which here means "perception" and "awareness," a gradual or sudden flash of truth, understanding or comprehension of something. Self-realization is self-knowing, understanding of the initial nature of true "I." Another meaning of this word is "fulfillment" – fulfillment of something that was previously only imagined. The word "realization" developed from the French "réaliser" – "to make real."

The sound of Anahat Naad is a seed planted by Shiva-Time in the womb of the Void.

—— **19** ——

गोरख उवाच

स्वामीजी, कौण परचे माया मोह छूटे,
कौण परचे शशि सूर फूटे ।
कौण परचे लागे बंध,
कौण परचे अजरावर कंध ॥

Gorakh says:

Swami ji, what knowledge dissolves illusion?
With what knowledge can moon and sun
                                                be pierced?
What knowledge can help to apply a lock (*bandh*)?
What knowledge makes the body immortal?

─── **20** ───

श्री मच्छन्द्र उवाच

अवधू! मन परचे माया मोह छूटे,
पवन परचे शशि घर फूटे ।
कान परचे लागे बंध,
गुरु परचे अजरावर कंध ॥

Shri Machhendra says:

**Avadhu! Illusion disappears with realization
of mind.**

**The house of moon is destroyed with realization
of breath.**

**A dam (*bandh*) can be applied with the help
of [true] hearing.**

**Body can become immortal with knowing
the Guru (*guru parche*).**

Illusion disappears with realization of mind

∿ Previously known reality dissolves when mind realizes it-self; the world as it was known to the practitioner ceases to exist.

When subconsciousness is "broken" and merged with its conscious half, they irreversibly transform each other.

As the result of this union, pure consciousness occurs and remains. In this new state of transformed and merged "non-dual" consciousness, the seeker will realize that the entire reality, the whole surrounding material world, expresses only forms perceived by mind.

The sadhak finds confirmation of this phenomenon wherever he focuses his newly attentive mind.

A dam (bandh) can be applied with the help of [true] hearing

The true hearing, or realization of the sound of Naad together with the words of Guru, stops the river of consciousness.

In yogic terms, "dam building," or application of a bandh, controls the tremendous current of mental and pranic energy.

Body can become immortal with knowing the Guru (guru parche)

Real knowledge (gyan) prevents deterioration of mind; realization of the teaching grants immortality.

Here the discussion reaches its peak.

Knowing the Guru allows one to meet, understand and realize one's own Atma, or never-dying spirit inside.

Real knowledge can be obtained only through meeting this Guru, through and by recognition of one's own Atma.

With the true knowledge, the discovery of immortal soul will make a striking impact on the gross body, granting immortality to its carrier.

Applied knowledge is the dam which stops the decay of mind and indulgence. The ageing of physical body will be reversed at the moment of true realization of one's own Atma.

The house of moon is destroyed with realization of breath

We already know that mind is referred to as "moon" in all yogic texts, and crescent moon is recognized as a symbol of immortality.

The science of Kriya Yoga points at the shape of crescent moon, which appears in the inner cavity behind the upper soft palate during the performance of Khechari Mudra, as discussed previously. Engaging the body and its organs in the physicality of sadhana, the yogi initiates the sublime metaphysics of mind transformation.

This yogic practice grants the nectar of immortality, as indicated in numerous yogic treatises and references to this secret mudra. When the practitioner realizes the metaphysics of the process, it will affect him on the physical plane. The effect of Khechari Mudra in combination with achieved breath control "pierces" the mind, eventually erasing its duality and granting a higher state of consciousness.

Vital breath is the only link, a unique connecting bridge between the physical body and the spirit which resides in it.

Only when firm control over breath has been gained, breath can take the practitioner to the Guru – one's own Atma.

Old manuscripts give a great description associated with this practice: being lost in the total darkness of Samsara, one can find a way out only by holding on to the thin thread of one's own breath, which will lead towards the light.

Take hold of your breath and come out of the darkness.

गोरख उवाच

स्वामीजी! कहां बसे मन कहां बसे पवन,
कहाँ बसे शब्द कहां बसे चंद।
कौण स्थान ए तत रहे,
सतगुरु होय सो पूछ्याँ कहै॥

Gorakh says:

Swami ji! Where does mind reside?

Where does breath dwell?

Where does word (*shabd*) live?

Where does moon reside?

Where do the essential elements (*tat*) exist?

You are the true Guru, kindly answer the question.

— 22 —

श्री मच्छन्द्र उवाच

अवधू! हृदय बसे मन, नाभी बसे पवन,
रूपे बसे शब्द गगन बसे चंद्र ।
अर्ध स्याने ए तत रहे,
ऐसा विचार मच्छन्द्र कहै ॥

Shri Machhendra says:

Avadhu! Mind resides in the heart;
Breath dwells in the navel (*naabhi*) center.
Word (*shabd*) lives in the form;
Moon resides in space (*gagan*).
These tattvas [essence of reality] dwell
in the middle.
Thus opinion utters Machhendra.

 Let's remind ourselves again who is giving answers and who is questioning, who is the Guru and who is the disciple? Matsyendranath converses with Gorakhnath, who has just attained immortality. Guru guides him to move further, beyond bodily limits.

Victory over death is the biggest achievement of yoga. Yet even physically immortal body remains gross by nature, and all the greatness of subtle mind dwelling inside the indestructible shell awaits to be discovered by the achiever.

There is no use of immortality if metaphysical realms and their mysteries remain unreachable and unexplored, if the physical body becomes immortal, but the mind inhibiting it remains inert.

The ultimate goal is to use an advanced state of immortality to develop an advanced mind, so that the very nature of this Creation and Its Creator can be understood by this new super-consciousness.

Mind resides in the heart

Myriads of emotions dwell in the heart, the epicenter of emotional powers; true feelings always emerge from the heart, not from the mind.

Void of the heart has to be discovered in the course of yogic sadhana: it shelters Prana and it is the abode of Vasudev. Heart opening technique in Kriya Yoga allows the practitioner to enter the Hriday (heart) center.

The true control of mind becomes a reality only upon successful piercing of Hriday granthi (passage of the "heart knot"). The symbolism of this term points at various mental "knots" accumulated during past and present life experiences. It can be safely stated that these knots (granthi) are limitations of our mind and consciousness.

In a way, our consciousness is tied and entangled in four major knots: in the course of yogic practice one has to cut through them and free the mind, letting it flow. The four knots are: Jivha (throat), Hriday (heart), Nabhi (navel) and Muladhara (root) granthi.

During Kriya practice, the sadhak successively passes through these knots, moving down from the top. Khechari, or the throat granthi, has to be passed first, then the yogi "unties" the granthi of the heart center. Piercing of Nabhi (the navel center) comes next, and finally, Muladhara granthi will be opened.

Breath dwells in the navel (naabhi) center

Translated into English as "navel," the Hindi word "naabhi" carries a complex meaning: it actually indicates the "center of life" or the "main vital point," not a tummy with a belly button.

The human embryo starts its development from this triggering center of life: a fetus breathes and receives nutrition while being connected to the mother through the navel.

Initial vital breath of an unborn child starts from this center and resides there till the moment of birth.

It may sound like a joke, but it is quite a serious matter: in the first seconds after a newborn emerges from the mother's body, the doctor slaps him/her to take the first breath through the mouth and lungs, interrupting the navel breathing and "switching" the newly arrived human to the common mode of oxygen intake.

The key to the real breath is embedded and hidden in the navel center: if the practitioner is able to "switch on" the type of breath via navel center, then the possibility of eternal life in one's body becomes a reality.

Word (shabd) lives in the form

The world begins by the will of God, or Absolute consciousness, the will of Shiva, expressed in the form of the Sound. Another definitive term for "will" is *Ichha Shakti*.

Shiva Sutras commentaries compare will to Uma Kumari, the most beautiful virgin... To obtain real willpower, or Ichha Shakti, to win Uma Kumari's heart is not an easy task.

The power to obtain and exercise this will is direct grace from Shakti; only She gives a gift of will in its totality.

Machhendranath states that Sound resides in form – any form. All given forms, objects and shapes were manifested by the vibration of Sound; form occurs whenever vibration of Anahat Naad condenses.

Moon resides in space (gagan)

Throughout this dialog, one question is repeated continuously in different variations: "Where does moon reside?"

Moon-mind dwells in space (gagan), heaven, sky, Akash, or Void, whose main property is Shabd – the everlasting Anahat Naad.

These tattvas [essence of reality] dwell in the middle

Tattva is the essence of Matter and Reality, the essence of Time and Prana.

This line refers to the median channel Sushumna, through which Prana as awakened Kundalini ascends to Sahasrara.

Initially, the body "receives" life force through the navel to start the process of physical growth; gradually Prana-Time develops the body to withstand the strong current of energy through Sushumna; at the peak of its rise, super-mind will be recognized by the carrier. Infused into Sushumna, Prana will give a gift of awareness of the tattva, the essence of Time.

Contemplation on the tattva of Time is possible only for highly developed consciousness, nurtured by the body.

23

गोरख उवाच

स्वामीजी! हृदय न होता तब कहां होता मन,
नाभी न होती तब कहां रहता पवन ।
रूप न होता तब कहां रहता शब्द,
गगन न होता तब कहाँ रहता चंद्र ॥

Gorakh says:

Swami ji! If there were no heart,
Where would mind reside?
Were there no navel center,
Where would breath live?
Were there no form, where would word reside?
If there were no space, where would moon be?

24

श्री मच्छन्द्र उवाच

अवधू! हृदय न होता तब शुन रहता मन,
नाभी न होती तब निरमल निरंकार होता पवन ।
रूप न होता तब शुन्नि रहता शब्द,
गगन न होता तब अन्तरिक्ष रहता चंद ॥

Shri Machhendra says:

Avadhu! If there were no heart,
Mind would reside in the Void (*shun*).
Were there no navel center,
Breath would live pure, without a form.
If there were no form, word (*shabd*)
                would reside in the Void.
Were there no space, moon
                would reside in the Void (*antariksh*).

From the beginning of times, Prana has been identified with individual Atma. Sun, Moon, Time, Mind and Atman are considered to possess similar archetypal qualities as Prana: everlasting renewal and cyclic recurrence of the movement.

Prana's function (to carry out the creation and annihilation, inhale and exhale) takes its roots in the self-sufficiency of the Absolute Consciousness of Time.

"Prana infills Prana, Prana infills creation (visarga). Constantly infilling it, Prana remains in the chests of the living."

(Svachanda Tantra)

In some yogic texts, Divine Consciousness is described as a flow of Prana carried by three nadis, as a dwelling place of sun, moon and fire and as aspects of Time:

"Highest, subtle, omnipresent Shakti, the essence of bliss and immortality, Mahaghoreshvari, Chanda, she creates and destroys. She holds three nullas of three types and three aspects [of time] ."

(Vajasaneya Tantra)

Array of questions and answers in these shlokas illuminates its qualities and nature.

If there were no heart, mind would reside in the Void (shun)

Aside from its physiological importance, the heart center, or Hriday, is also known as one of the several substitutes of the concept of "Absolute Consciousness," or Universal Heart.

The term "hriday" itself means the "pit where Prana lives."

Concentrated in the heart center, Prana is recognized as the universal principle of Life which pervades all things around us. Animating the body via breath force, Prana is the main attribute of Life and the indicator of the carrier's consciousness.

A concealed potential form of life and its dynamics exist even in a dead body, as decay is just another transformational stage of life force. But the phenomenon of Prana grants Life to bodies in its most dynamic form, sustaining consciousness.

Presence of Prana in human hearts is compared to numerous reflections of the sun in the myriads of different water bowls: the source is one.

And individual vital breath acts as a single link and the only connection with the outer source of life force, Universal Prana, and its "reflection" which inhibits every living heart.

Yogic control of breath, or established connection with Prana, allows the practitioner to move his conscious mind beyond the carbon-based creation. Led by pranic force, his consciousness will merge with the consciousness of Time Itself.

Willing to explore the distant and unknown, a yogi starts from within and submerges into his own heart. Holding on to the breath, he realizes Prana in Hriday center and moves his mind together with Prana to its cosmic source.

Only personal practice and individual experience can get the practitioner closer to the Universal Heart.

A phenomenon of this world, Prana originated on another plane, which lies beyond the carbon-based creation; it belongs to the infinity of Time (Shiva, or Purush).

Being part of this creation, we represent it with our own bodies, hearts and minds; if we are able to realize Prana inside our hearts and establish a direct connection to its universal source, then we can connect different planes and dimensions only by will of mind and mastery of breath.

This process can be compared with fetal development: after it has reached its fullest potential in the womb, it will not remain inside, it will emerge into the outer "dimension."

When the yogi's physical and mental development reaches its peak, he will leave the womb of this realm and, following Prana into the Void, will reach Moksha.*

---

* Liberation from rebirth.

If there were no form, word (shabd) would reside in the Void

Shabd-word lives in the Void, expressing and manifesting itself in the form of sound, Naad, only by the will of Time, or Shiva.

Time itself has no point of origin, lineage or family, cast or varna – its roots are unknown; it is formless and unattainable.

The shapeless sound – Anahat Naad – resides in the Void, being a seed of Time; it does not depend on any other carrier but Universal Emptiness.

The next shlokas explain what happens in the absence of carriers to the key element which unites them all.

the *TWILIGHT LANGUAGE of GORAKH BODH*

--- **25** ---

गोरख उवाच

स्वामीजी! रात्रि होती दिन कहां ते आया,
दिन होते रात्रि कहां समावे ।
दीवा बुझाना ज्योति कहां लिया बास,
पिंड न होता तब कहां प्राण का निवास ॥

Gorakh says:

Swami ji! If there were night, then where would
day come from?
If there were day, where would night sink from?
When a lamp is extinguished, where
does light dwell?
If there were no physical body (*pind*), then where
would Prana reside?

श्री मच्छन्द्र उवाच

अवधू राति होती दिन सहजे आया,
दिन प्रकाशै राति सहज समाया।
दिवा बुझाना ज्योति निरंतर बास,
पिंड न होता तब प्राण का शुन्न निवास॥

Shri Machhendra says:

Avadhu! Were there night, day would
come naturally (*sahaj*).
Were there daylight shining, night would
sink naturally.
When a lamp is extinguished, the light [still]
dwells permanently.
If there were no physical body, Prana would
reside in the Void.

Changes of day and night are perceptible only to inhabitants of Earth affected by the cycles of planetary rotation; such perception of time is irrelevant in the Void, in the outer space.

By extending itself beyond restraints of its earthly body and realizing the Void, mind detaches itself from the pre-conditioned state and changes its previously limited perception of time.

No longer constrained by the limitations of the body, consciousness moves away and enters the Void.

The state of stabilized consciousness, which already tolerated and experienced every possible emotion and experience and is no longer affected by an external impact, is called "Sahaj."

The metamorphoses of such a mind can be compared to daylight, which absorbs the darkness of night with natural easiness: it is simply a property of day to replace night.

In the same way, effortless merging of conscious and subconscious minds (comparable with day and night) leads to the state of pure Consciousness. Upon entering this state, the practitioner is able to recognize the Conscious Void.

In Its form of universal life force, Prana is yet another property of the Void; even in the absence of an individual physical body (vessel of the life force), Prana will continue to permeate Universal Emptiness.

Being the main connecting element, Prana is present in mind, breath, word or sound... Breath is incidental, but its root force, or the Univeral energy, which makes breathing possible, is immanent.

In the absence of individual carriers of Prana, life force would still exist in Shunya: breath in its purest form would return to the emptiness of the Void, to its source.

Vibration of the sound would still continue to inhibit primordial Emptiness even in the absence of individual receptacles; it would return to the source of its own origin, Bindu, back to the seed of Time.

With no shelter of physical heart, mind would unite with its origin, Universal Hriday, pulsating Absolute Consciousness, and would continue to exist in the form of Consciousness of the Void.

All these phenomena (day, night, breath) are different expressions of Prana, which inhibits numerous carriers (bodies, hearts etc.) that belong to the Void; existing in various forms and retaining their subjective individuality, they are at the same time part of the Conscious Shunya.

The primal source and universal origin, Void will continue to exist regardless of existence of carriers of its essence, Prana.

---— 27/MSP* —---

गोरख उवाच

स्वामीजी! काया का कौण कर्ता, कथं तेज उपाया ।
ब्रह्म ज्ञान का कौण सद् गुरु शिष्य होई,
कौण अलख लखाया ॥

Gorakh says:

Swami ji! Who is the creator of the body (*kaya*)?
Where can effulgence (*tej*) be found?
Who is a true guru and disciple of Divine
knowledge (*brahma gyaan*)?**
Who can make the unseeable visible?

---

* Nine shlokas are absent from the source manuscript ("Shree Gorakh Bodh Vani Sangrah" by Swami Ramprakash Maharaj Agrawat) used in this publication as a reference Hindi text. However, they were present in Mohan Singh's work "Gorakhnath and Medieval Hindu Mysticism" (Lahore: Oriental College 1937). Their value supports the continuity of narration, and they are commented upon in this publication.

Such lines are marked as MSP (Mohan Singh Publication). For more information, see "Sources and References" on page 311.

---------- **28/MSP** ----------

श्री मच्छन्द्र उवाच

अवधू! काया का ब्रह्मा कर्ता, सत थैं तेज उपाया ।
ब्रह्मा ज्ञान का सुनि सद् गुरु शिष्य है अलख लखाया ॥

Shri Machhendra says:

Avadhu! The Supreme Mind (*brahma*) is
the creator of the body.
In truth effulgence can be found.
The Void is the true guru and disciple
of Divine knowledge (*brahma gyaan*).
They [Satguru and disciple] can make the
unseeable visible [through their realization].

☙ By realizing the Void, who is both Guru and disciple of all existing things, the sadhak is able to see the invisible essence of reality. Out of the Void comes the unobstructed sound of Anahat Naad. If a yogi develops an ability to hear this sound – then he will be able to understand that the Greater Mind is the creator of the "kaya" ("body").

The Supreme Mind creates a body so it can be impregnated with the seed of consciousness, so it can finally take birth in the given body.

Through that birth of consciousness comes the light of Satya, Light of the Truth.

They [Satguru and disciple] can make the unseeable visible [through their realization]

Modern science researches and tests particles inhibiting the void but does not emphasize the importance of the Void Itself sufficiently. It is the carrier of all Universal Matter and the source of Universal Sound, Sound of the Truth, the name of the Creator... This sound, this name, this truth continuously emanates from the Void, appearing again and again.

Consciousness remains unseen inside the body created by mind, whose source is the Void. Void can be comprehended and experienced only by invisible consciousness dwelling in the Void's very creation – earthly body.

No one has ever seen the Void or the Consciousness, but they are experienced every moment by means of bodies and minds.

Being introduced by the Satguru to the Conscious Void, the yogi will reach the source of the Sound, the point of Its emanation; maybe there the seeker will meet the Greater Mind, Creator Brahma, face to face and become one with It.

The unseen can be witnessed through a seeker's realization granted by a Guru.

But who is this Guru?

Naths always addressed yogic mind as developed consciousness in its totality. Born out of persistent practice of pranayamas, fragments of consciousness (Manas, Buddhi and Ahamkara) will unite in the act of deliverance as *pragya*, highly developed intellect.

Such a mind is able to cognize the sound of Anahat Naad, such a mind can become the student of Atma, in such a body Guru-spirit and chela-mind unite and become one.

There will be time when the inner guru – controlled breath-Prana itself – will start teaching Atma. After some time, hard practice will change their status and relationship: Teacher-breath will become an eager student led by spirit-Atma.* Upon recognition of their unity, they will stay in the body forever, granting immortality to it.

Generally, our intellect relies on memories, bygone experiences and stored database of knowledge obtained by previous generations. Intellectual abilities to identify, analyze and determine the essence of objects or meaning of events are firmly rooted in our past.

Translated as "knowledge," gyan is the received and stored information. Vigyan is experience of knowledge which was processed and absorbed individually. By living by, with and through gyan-knowledge, one transforms it into vigyan-wisdom.

However, pragya is an ability of a developed mind to face phenomena, appearance of ideas or facts without reaching into the library of the past, without addressing memories or experiences. It is an ability to immediately and directly cognize without "re-cognition."

This happens due to the realization of unity of Satguru-spirit and its disciple-mind, and that's how the unseeable becomes visible, and that's where yogic practice should take inquiring Atma.

---

* See shloka 79 for more information about this process.

29

गोरख उवाच

स्वामीजी! काया मध्ये के लख चंद,
पुहुप मध्ये कहां बसे गंध।
दूध मध्ये कहां बसे घीव,
पिन्ड मध्ये कहाँ बसे जीव॥

Gorakh says:

Swami ji! How many moons are there
in the body?

Where does fragrance reside in a flower?

Where is melted butter (*ghee*) concealed in milk?

Where does the soul (*jiv*) dwell in the body?

30

श्री मच्छन्द्र उवाच

अवधू! काया मध्ये दूबेला चंद्र,
पुहुप मध्ये चेतन गंध।
दूध मध्ये निरंतर घीव,
पिंड मध्ये सर्व व्यापक जीव॥

Shri Machhendra says:

Avadhu! There are two moons in the body.

Consciousness (*chetan*) is the fragrance
 [manifested] in the flower.

Ghee is permanently in milk.

Soul pervades all over the body.

There are two moons in the body

൭ Two eyes reflect the mind, its conscious and unconscious components.

Evenly spread throughout the body, Atma, or the soul, is not centralized; united with Prana, it flows through nadis.

During its journey, Atma internalizes all intellectual knowledge, every intuitive guess and grain of emotion, absorbing every single touch, gaze and feeling, sudden understanding or recognition.

But where does the soul conceal itself?

Presence of spirit, or jiva, in the body is similar to ghee (melted butter) concealed in milk: existing in every drop of milk, it remains unseen.

In order to extract and separate butter from milk, one has to initiate a long and laborious process of transformation.

In the same way yoga directs the body, just like unprocessed milk, to go through many transformations so that jiva can be educed, so it can shine alone, distinct in all its potential. Concentrated and crystallized as a result of the yogic process, such jiva is recognized as the immortal substance of the body.

Consciousness (chetan) is the fragrance [manifested] in the
flower. Ghee is permanently in milk.
Soul pervades all over the body

Consciousness is jiva's fragrance and sole evidence of existence: if we are alive – we are conscious (and vice versa). Presence of consciousness in the body is the sole confirmation of the very fact of being alive.

Atma embraces Prana inside each cell of the body, making us fully aware of our own existence: vivid and active, consciousness confirms the fact of life to us...

Mind is an expression of Atma, empowered with limitless potential for development. To instigate this process, Atma needs to be recognized first. Recognition requires the highest level of inner awareness and sensitivity: only developed attentiveness gives the first glimpse of unseeable and allows learning of unknowable.

The word "consciousness" is used frequently, but hardly a few people are able to understand its meaning in full. It should not be confused with intellect (Buddhi), as its intellectual abilities are just some of the countless facets of consciousness.

The best description of consciousness still belongs to Machhendranath, who compared it with the fragrance of the flower.

गोरख उवाच

स्वामीजी! काया न होती तब कहां रहता सूरज चंद ।
पहुप न होता तव कहां रहता गंध ।
दूध नहीं होता तब कहां रहता घीव ।
काया न होती तब कहां रहता जीव ॥

Gorakh says:

Swami ji! Were there no body, where would sun
and moon reside?

Were there no flower, where would fragrance
dwell?

Were there no milk, where would ghee exist?

Were there no body, where would the spirit
reside?

—————————————— 32/MSP ——————————————

श्री मच्छन्द्र उवाच

अवधू! काया न होती तव निरंतरि रहता सूरज चंद्र ।
पहुप नहीं होता तव अनहद् रहता गंध ।
दूध न होता तव सुनि रहता घीव ।
काया न होती तव प्रम सुनि रहता जीव ॥

Shri Machhendra says:

Avadhu! Were there no body, sun and moon
would reside in Eternity (*nirantari*).
If there were no flower, fragrance would dwell
in Anahad [Naad].
Were there no milk, ghee would reside
in the Void.
If there were no body, the spirit would reside
in the Supreme Void (*param shunn*).

༄ Individual mind continuously confirms the fact of existence, assuring the soul of it. But what would happen with consciousness in the absence of an individual carrier?

Reflection of the Moon or the Sun can be seen in a bowl of water, but the existence of these planets does not depend on their reflections in the bowl.

The light of God is reflected in each one of us, but the existence of God does not depend on these reflections. It means a world to us, but to Him it is only a "play of shadows," a speckle of reflection of His glory.

Throw water out of the bowl – and even then the Sun and the Moon will continue to exist. Destroy the body – and jiva will still be present. Cut the flower – its essence and fragrance will remain in the air, the carrier of all fragrances and smells. Fragrance was already in existence and the flower is just a means of its expression. Singing, recitation of a melody, performance of a symphony or raga are just various interpretations of music of the Void, present everywhere: the humanity tries to express this omnipotent and omnipresent sound with suitable tools.

Written notes indicate a musical code, but they will be recognized as music only when played and expressed by the sound of voice or instrument.

Written musical keys are not music but an indication toward it.

Those who have been taught to accept only written musical notes may never acknowledge singing or the sound of violin as real music; they will never agree that sounds express symbols on pages.

Our thoughts are formless; when an idea takes the shape of a spoken word, it becomes a power sealing an expression of mind. An initially formless thought still dwells in the background of mind, remaining there as the essense and true origin of the spoken word.

A written word gains even more power, but the initial essence of a formless thought sometimes disappears in letters.

Only symbols remain on pages and the humanity continues to collect and worship them as the ultimate truth-bearing signs.

Reading books of yoga, we go too deep into the printed code of letters and words, forgetting about the real essence of its ancient wisdom.

Human bodies and consciousness inhibiting them are direct indications of existence of Greater Reality, Endless Void. Every movement of mind, every thought and every idea points toward it; we should try to understand it and train our mind to look at Its deceivingly distant horizon.

गोरख उवाच

स्वामीजी! कहाँ बसे चंद् कहां बसे सूर,
कहां बसे नाद् बिंद् का मूर,
कहां चढि हंसा पीवे पाणी,
कौण शक्ति प्राण घर आणी ॥

Gorakh says:

Swami ji! Where does moon reside;
Where does sun reside?
Where does sound (*naad*) dwell?
Where is the origin of Bindu?*
Where does swan (*hansa*) ascend to drink water?
Which power (*shakti*) brings breath (*praan*) home?

---

* Bindu is the point at which creation starts; it is the sacred symbol of the universe in its unmanifested state.

──────────── **34** ────────────

श्री मच्छन्द्र उवाच

अवधू! उर्ध बसे चन्द अर्ध बसे सूर,
हृदय बसे नाद बिंद जो मूर।
गगन चढ़ि हंसा पीवे पाणी,
उलटि शक्ति आप धरि आणी॥

Shri Machhendra says:

Avadhu! Moon resides atop (*urdh*);
Sun resides in the middle (*ardh*).
Sound (*naad*) dwells in the heart (*hriday*).
Bindu itself is origin.
Swan [of the soul] ascends to heaven (*gagan*)
                                to drink water.
Reversed power (*ulti shakti*) grasps self and
                                returns [to itself].

〜 Moon is Prana, Shiva, inhaled breath; Sun is Apana, Shakti, exhalation of energy.

Swan [of the soul] ascends to heaven (gagan) to drink water

At the time of death, Hans-breath flies away from the body, but a yogi enters the state of breathlessness and experiences death-like state of Samadhi willingly, by the power of practice and grace of the Guru.

An old Indian belief says that all swans-souls fly to Lake Mansarovar to drink from it and take pearls of wisdom. Hans-jiva satisfies its thirst in the lake of mind.

When a yogi enters the breathless state and steps into the Void, led by the sound of Naad, then Hans (captured Prana – retained vital breath) drinks the nectar of knowledge from the stillness of mind. This highly poetic comparison describes exact results of yogic sadhana.

Sound (naad) dwells in heart (hriday)

Spanda, or initial vibration, is the pulse of the Absolute Consciousness of Time, Its dynamic force and initial triggering point of creation.

Cosmic vibration of Anahat Naad emanates from Bindu, a formless point without dimensions or coordinates.

It is the origin of the entire creation, the source of all manifested Matter, conceived in the womb of the Void.

Born out of Spanda, or the throb of Absolute Mind via Bindu, primordial Sound-Naad is the cause of creation; that's why it is called the root of the world.

When Naad's vibration condenses, it produces material world known to us.

Everything around us is a manifestation of Spanda, expressed by a condensed vibration of sound, as all gross Matter is born out of it.

As discussed above, "heart" indicates an organ of the physical body, but the word "hriday" refers to the place inhibited by the essence of life, Prana. In yoga, Hriday symbolizes Prana and its dwelling place.

Only in the breathless condition swan-Hans, or the breath, will find rest in the Void and will become aware of vibration emanating from bindu, which dwells there. By flying with Sound-Naad, Hans will reach Bindu, the essence of the entire creation. From this moment, a different type of consciousness will emerge.

Reversed power (ulti shakti) grasps self and returns [to itself]

These lines describe a breathless condition in the state of suspended animation, achieved by mastered control over breath and, consequently, over the vital life force, Prana-Kundalini.

The spinal cord of human embryo starts to develop from the same center as the brain, progressing further. Kundalini energy sleeps at the end of this extension, at the root base of the spine.

To reverse the power of creation, which formed the physical body and planted Kundalini energy at the base of the spinal cord, a yogi redirects the flow of vital energy towards the brain – the initial source of its origin. By the power of breath control, the yogi moves unified Prana-Apana to that source, infusing it into Sushumna; Kundalini rides this flow, moving upwards, to the upper chakra.

We might speculate that, transformed by their union, Prana and Apana gain new properties, **becoming Kundalini** Herself.

Upon replacement of Apana with the power of Prana, the flow of conscious mind replaces subconsciousness, awakening it and revealing its true origin.

Reversal of power to its own source is not a reflection of experience but the direct perception of truth.

गोरख उवाच

स्वामीजी! कहाँ उत्पत्ति ते नाद,
कहाँ नाद समि भवते।
कौण ले स्थापिते नाद,
कहां नाद विलियते॥

Gorakh says:

Swami ji! Where does sound (*naad*)
                                            originate from?
Where does sound exist in equipoise (*sam*)?
What can establish sound?
Where does sound disappear to?

36

श्री मच्छन्द्र उवाच

अवधू! औंकार उत्पत्ति ते नाद,
नाद शुभ सम भवति ।
पवन ले स्थापिते नाद,
नाद निरंजन विलियते ॥

Shri Machhendra says:

Avadhu! The sound (*naad*) emerges from
    [the sound of] Om (*omkaar*).

The sound [Naad] balances in equipoise
    [in the Void] auspiciously.

Establish sound through [tuning]
    the vital breath [with it].

The Sound merges in the formless (*niranjan**).

〜 Vital breath is the key to this shloka. By stopping the breath, the sadhak enters another dimension.

The sound (naad) emerges from [the sound of] Om (omkaar)

An ordinary mind is conditioned by imprints of old memories, applied dogmas and common beliefs; such a mental state clouds and blocks the awareness of Naad.

---

* The state of Niranjan lies beyond the boundaries of this creation based on the element of carbon, beyond this realm.

To hear the soundless Anahat Naad, mind has to become unconditional: only then one will become aware of this cosmic sound.

The simplicity of this statement might escape us, as we are fitted to required standards from the very beginning, which prevents the mind from gaining totality.

But how can mind become unconditional?

The sound of Naad is heard at the time of death or right after death, when Atma is no longer bound to the physical body.

Continuous yogic practice is extremely important: consistent attempts to experience Naad during life prepare the sadhak for the immediate after-death experience.

The main goal for any Atma is to recognize the source of its own existence in this cosmic sound and light; yogic practice is a tool for this recognition.

Imagine the splendor of thousands of suns and simultaneous roar of thousands of lions, imagine the mighty sound of thunder and myriads of ocean waves breaking into the shore...

An extreme fear will overwhelm those who have never experienced it while living – and any attempt to escape from it will be the end of spiritual progress. A slim possibility of spiritual journey will end without even starting.

By the grace of Guru and by the power of persistent yogic practice, the seeker experiences the cosmic sound daily while still inhibiting his physical body. He will not be afraid of the blinding splendor of light and terrifying roar of Naad.

He will embrace the amazement and bliss of realization and will move to the source of creation, origin of his own life and the entire universe.

Yoga emphasizes the great importance of practice of Yoni Mudra: it allows the practitioner to experience the great Naad and to see the splendor of its light daily.

Every time in Yoni Mudra the yogi meets a little death, preparing for the after-death experience and for the chance to recognize the source of his own jiva and merge with it. This secret practice makes Kriya the most powerful and mysterious of all yogic paths.

Matsyendranath instructs Gorakhnath to stop his breath and firmly install himself in Naad. The listener merges with the Sound; his own form will vanish, along with the mental conceptualization of materiality of the world. The sadhak will begin to identify himself with Naad, taking a step toward the formless, dissolving his mind in it; there will be no more duality.

गोरख उवाच

स्वामीजी! नादे न नादिबा बिंदे न बिंदवा,
गगने न लाईबा आशा।
नाद बिंद दोऊ न होईगा,
तब प्राण का कहां होइगा बासा ॥

Gorakh says:

Swami ji! If sound (*naad*) did not clang,
if Bindu did not exist,
If space (*gagan*) did not bring hope,
If there were neither sound nor Bindu,
Then where would Prana reside?

38

श्री मच्छन्द्र उवाच

अवधू! नादे भी नादिवा बिंदवा,
बिंदवा गगने दिलाईबा आशा।
नाद बिन्द दोऊ न होईगा,
तब प्राण पुरुष का विरंतरि होईगा बासा॥

Shri Machhendra says:

Avadhu! The sound clangs and Bindu exists.
The existence of Bindu compels space
to bring hope.
If there were neither sound nor Bindu,
Then Prana would eternally reside in
Purush [Shiva, or the Time].

The sound clangs and Bindu exists.
The existence of Bindu compels space to bring hope

೧ The initial source of creation, Bindu is omnipresent. The unstruck sound of Naad emanates from Bindu's multiplicity ubiquitously and simultaneously.

Omnipotent, present everywhere and nowhere at the same time, Bindu is not stable or fixed.

Its movements are both internal and external. This movement is dance-like – that's why Shiva is depicted as Nataraja, Lord of the Cosmic Dance.

The very sublime will is the first emergence of the conscious mind; without initial consciousness, will itself cannot be manifested.

Being a catalytic agent which connects elements of Matter with the Void, Consciousness came from Shunya.

The moment when the Universal Mind starts connecting Eternal Emptiness with manifestation of material world is when the first hope and desire to explore unknown reality is born.

This initial movement of Consciousness is a hope to know, to learn about this new material world in its totality. Technically, this willingness to discover and hope for knowing is called a sublime desire.

When Consciousness registers and connects the fact of formation of Matter by the Void, witnessing the creation of Life, it experiences curiosity and the desire to study and experience this newly formed phenomenon of materiality. And that is how Samsara begins.

Every specific hope and desire is an urge to experience life in its particular form, to study it from a certain angle. For us, humans, our desires and hopes are the main criteria and confirmation of being alive and present in this material world. Consciousness itself is a hope to experience life.

If there were neither sound nor Bindu,
Then Prana would eternally reside in Purush [Shiva, or the
Time]

It is worth repeating: the cosmic sound of Naad emanates from the vibration of Bindu. Condensed Naad is the basis and method of manifestation of the material world.

Modern science agrees that this world was born out of vibration; our bodies materialized as a result of condensed resonance of the primal sound, which had emanated from the universal point of creation – Bindu.

Born out of the same reverberation which manifests our creation, we are constantly experiencing it in a vast variety of differently expressed forms: walls, trees and bridges, birds and animals, oceans and deserts...

But this creation does not extend beyond the limits of vibration of Anahat Naad and its source of origin.

With carbon being the essence and basis of this creation, our world in its entirety is confined within the boundaries of carbon-based environment.

Beyond its edges lies the state of Alakh Niranjan, the state beyond carbon, and that is where Consciousness of Time begins.

Omnipresent in the carbon-based world, Prana does not depend on its existence, nor is it conditioned by Bindu, from which this world had emanated. Bindu itself is the seed of Time planted in the womb of the Void.

Outspread beyond the world of carbon, Prana is eternally merged with Param Purush, or Shiva, whose other names are Time and the universal essence of life, or Prana itself.

It spreads beyond the Void (which is Shakti, the female aspect of creation) to reunite with the seed-giving Time (Shiva).

The creative and life-bearing nature, Shakti-Prakriti ("nature") is Void Itself, or, rather, Nature is part of it. Going beyond the boundaries of Void (Shakti-Prakriti-Nature), Prana urges to re-unite with its eternal source, Shiva-Purush-Time. Time and Void form ultimate primordial Duality.

To understand the cosmic creation of galaxies, let's imagine Time and Void merged together (this form of union can also be called "Ardhanarishvara") in the temporary state of non-duality. Unavoidable separation follows, but the seed of Time, Bindu, starts to vibrate in the womb of the Void, giving birth to the Matter. Time impregnates the Void with the seed of creation; the newborn creation is already dual by nature.

Being a property of this creation, duality never ends, but a true seeker may develop an ability to appraise its limits and cross its borders.

Such an ability can be described as transformation of conscious mind into its subconscious state; by sustaining this state, the seeker understands higher aspects of universal dichotomy.

Only by crossing the boundaries of one state, the yogi can truly see, appraise and remain aware of totality which contains both of them.

गोरख उवाच

स्वामीजी! आकार छूटसी निराकार होवसी,
पवन न होसी पाणी ।
चंद सूर दोऊ नहीं होसी,
तब हँस की कौण निशाणी ॥

Gorakh says:

Swami ji! If form vanished and the formless
appeared;
If there were no breath, no water;
If there were neither moon nor sun,
Then where would the swan's landing spot be?

---- **40** ----

श्री मच्छन्द्र उवाच

अवधू! सहज हँस का खेल भणीजे,
शुन्य हँस का वासा ।
सहज ही आकार निराकार होसी,
परम ज्योति हँस का निवासा ॥

Shri Machhendra says:

Avadhu! Spontaneity appears as a play
of the swan (*hans*).

Void is the swan's dwelling.

Form becomes formless effortlessly
and naturally (*sahaj*).

The Supreme Light (*param jyoti*) is the abode of
the swan.

ᐁ In these lines the shloka describes the highest level of achievement: when developed consciousness has overcome physical confinements and limitations of the body and the yogi begins to see beyond the forms of given reality.

When Hans, or vital breath, is retained, body is compared to a pot filled with still air. As long as Prana remains inside, the life of the body continues. The ability to "fill the pot" of the body ("kumbh") with vital air and keep it there without inhaling or exhaling is called the state of Sahaj Kumbhak or Keval Kumbhak.* This state marks the climax of yogic practice.

---

* See shloka 98 for more details on Keval Kumbhak.

Great tolerance, or the ability to withstand any condition, including breathlessness, is called "Sahaj." When breath-Hans effortlessly and naturally ("sahaj") enters a breathless state, it takes refuge in it. The flow of exhalation and inhalation is ceased, and Hans is able to nest in the captured stillness of retained air; there breath will naturally remain safe.

Form becomes formless effortlessly and naturally (sahaj).
The Supreme Light (param jyoti) is the abode of the swan

Param Jyoti, or the Supreme Light, is another name of Ishvara who dwells inside each heart.

The state of Paramhans, the Supreme Spirit, begins from the moment when breath-Hans agrees to remain with Param Jyoti instead of flying away, commemorating and establishing the soul of the Soul, the spirit of the Spirit.

Paramhans, the Supreme Swan, is the breath of the Breath, the light of the Light and the prana of the Prana.

Any gross surface able to reflect light is called form; we see materiality of the surrounding world in countless forms and formations. When light passes through any entity without producing any reflection, when no physicality or materiality is there to meet the light, then such a condition is called formless.

Departure from the mental concept of form into the formless state has a much deeper meaning than merely acceptance of a new identity: conscious and formless essence (universal Prana), which has always existed outside the body, enters it, infilling the mind with the Supreme Light of the Highest Reality.

The sadhak realizes that existence is not limited by the form of the body: he is able to be anywhere and take any form with his newly transformed mind.

The true beauty of formless state is in the power of consciousness, which enables the yogi to overcome the limitation of the form and take any shape at will.

We are neither the clothes on our bodies nor the bodies inside them.

गोरख उवाच

स्वामीजी! अमूल का कौणो मूल,
कहां का बास।
ता पद का गुरु कौण है
पूछत यति गोरखनाथ ॥

Gorakh says:

Swami ji! What is the root of the rootless
And where does the rootless reside?
Who is the Master *(guru)* of that place?
Thus asked Gorakhnath.

42

श्री मच्छन्द्र उवाच

अवधू! अमूल का शुन मूल है,
मूल निरंतर वास।
ता पद का निरवाण गुरु,
कथत मच्छन्द्र नाथ॥

Shri Machhendra says:

Avadhu! Void is the root of the rootless.
Root [Void] is its permanent abode.
Nirvana* is the Guru of that place [Void].
Thus says Machhendranath.

Void is the root of the rootless.
Root [Void] is its permanent abode

∽ Music is present in every note it consists of, but separate notes will not produce a melody. The analysis of dissected notes will not reveal the essence of the tune. Yogis accept Great Shunya as a cradle of Creation and abode of Time by starting recognition of the void in their own bodies and moving further, to cognition of the Void's totality.

Yet Void is not ultimate, but Time is. However, Universal Emptiness does not root in Time; they are interconnected, co-existing, permeating, supporting each other and blended together forever.

---

* Nirvana means liberation, cessation of physical existence.

Baseless and omnipresent, invisible and impalpable, Void holds and conceals the Matter, which has no other root but Emptiness Itself.

In the foreword to the commentary on *Shiva Sutra* I wrote: "Out of the union of conscious Time and conscious Void, conscious Matter takes birth."

Void and Time, Shiva and Shakti, produce universal Matter, the fabric of our material world.

In Sanskrit "void" literally means "shakti." We are conditioned to search for the "root" of existence, attempting to understand its origin, because our own roots are part of our identity and we are longing to know it.

Yes, it is hard to accept something beginningless, endless and rootless as the origin of our physical existence, yet such is the natural immensity of forces within and beyond our limits and measures.

Nirvana is the Guru of that place [Void]

The yogi achieves the main, primary and divine goal by superseding it. The Supreme Guna is the liberation, or Nirvana; it is the biggest goal, highest accomplishment and the Supreme Teacher.

Every tapas is aimed at entering the state of Nirvana. Being the ultimate and last attainment, Nirvana is compared with Guru, because in his great effort to reach it, the sadhak receives gyan of unmeasurable depth, learning from the Void.

The final destination and inspirational Guru, the Void leads the seeker to his destiny: in this quest the yogi enters Nirvana.

A liberated yogi will reach the state beyond Triguna; he will exist outside the effect of three gunas and will not be affected by karmas connected with them. Stepping beyond the limitations of nature,* he will overcome its effects.

Free in every aspect, with a single movement of his super-consciousness he will be able to create or annihilate his own universe.

All works by Swatmarama, Matsyendranath and Gorakhnath describe techniques aimed at overcoming the effects of old age. The purpose of practicing yoga is at least to be able to cross 120 years to become free of the influence of gunas.

For anyone who has crossed the age barrier of 120 years, the impact of planetary cycle is over as well as the influences of karmic effects; such a person will be liberated from all karmas.

He will be free to create a new future – if it is still desirable or physically possible.

After this age barrier is crossed, the person's mental state changes even if he has not achieved the state of Samadhi during his lifetime.

The very fact that Atma was able to spend 120 years in the same body grants an ability of truly free thinking.

But "Nirvana" and "Samadhi" are not synonyms, these states take an adept to distinctively different destinations. When a yogi

---

* Stepping beyond the limits of nature signifies successive steps of yogic practice: overcoming constraints of physical body, erasing all klesha (spiritual afflictions) and vasana (karmic tendencies) of former mental imprints and exiting the boundaries of carbon-based earthly realm.

decides to leave his physical body, which has already experienced thousands of Samadhis during his lifetime, instead of opting for immortality in such a body, then such a transition is called "attaining the state of Nirvana."

Such a decision is taken at the crossroads by those who have reached the heights of choosing their own future: to leave the body or to remain in it indefinitely.

If there is no option of immortality, then there is no possibility of achieving Nirvana and entering the Void.

गोरख उवाच

स्वामीजी! कहाँ ते उत्पत्ति प्राण,
कहाँ उत्पत्ति ते मन।
कहां उत्पत्ति ते वाचा,
कहां वाचा विलीयते॥

Gorakh says:

Swami ji! Where does Prana originate from?
Where does mind arise from?
Where does speech come from?
Where does speech disappear?

─────────── **44** ───────────

श्री मच्छन्द्र उवाच

अवधू! अवगति ते उत्पन्न प्राण,
प्राण उत्पत्ति ते मन ।
मन उत्पत्ति ते वाचा,
वाचा मन विलीयते ॥

Shri Machhendra says:

Avadhu! Prana arises from cognition
(*avagati*) [of the spirit].
Mind originates from Prana.
Speech comes from mind;
Speech disappears in mind.

Prana arises from cognition (avagati) [of the spirit]

෴ Cognition produces Prana. It emerges from recognition of the spirit and this is the beginning of knowledge.

Ignited by Prana, mind produces a formless thought; then the sound of speech carries it, shaping and expressing a formerly formless thought in the form of word.

Enriched by mind and expressed in the sound of speech, the thought becomes "conscious" (or spoken) and then dissolves in the mind again.

The more thoughts are born by mind and absorbed or received by it, the more powerful and potent consciousness becomes.

गोरख उवाच

स्वामीजी! कुसबद कु कुण ग्रसै, सुसवद का किथं वास।
द्वादश अंगुल वायु कुण मुखि रहै।
सतगुरु होई सो पूछया कहै ॥

Gorakh says:

Swami ji! What catches a bad word?
Where is the abode of a good word?
Where does the air of twelve fingers' [breadth]
reside?
You are the true Guru, kindly explain.

श्री मच्छन्द्र उवाच

अवधू! कुसवद कु सुसवद ग्रसै, सुसवद वा निरंतरि वास।
द्वादश अंगुल वायु गुरु मुखि रहै।
ऐसा विचार मच्छन्द्र कहै॥

Shri Machhendra says:

Avadhu! The good word catches the bad word;
The abode of the good word is Eternity (*nirantar*).
The air of twelve fingers' [breadth] resides in
                                   the Guru's mouth.*
Thus opinion utters Machhendra.

〜 Being the seed of all mantras, Om creates the sound
of Naad, which, in turn, serves as the very basis of all spoken
words; the divinity of Om swallows all other words (bad words).

"Om Tat Sat" ("It is That") is the main formula, which points at
Param Shiva, or the Highest Reality. Together with "So-Ham"
mantra, these words are practiced by the sadhaks who were
initiated to the highest (Paramhans) levels.

In another string of his later shabds (sayings), Goraksha says:

"*Breath thunders and breath echoes,*
Breath pierces six chakras and roams up and down
Breath flows through the body in the form of "*So-Ham*"
And "*Hamsa*" *mantras…*"

---

* Control of the vital breath, outflowing from the nostrils of practitioner at
    the length of twelve fingers is obtained by absorption of Guru's words.

The air of twelve fingers' [breadth] resides in the Guru's mouth

This line refers to the measure of the strength and length of exhalation and inhalation during pranayama performed by an initiated sadhak as directed by his Guru.

If breath exceeds that count, reaches the length beyond the distance of twelve fingers from the nose, then the body is believed to decay faster and the aging process gets speedy.

"End of twelve fingers' breadth," or *dvādaśānta*, refers to three different places. The first dvadasanta describes a spot outside the body as a distance at which breath dissolves (at the length of twelve fingers, or "three hands" from the nose).

The second type of dvadasanta is internal: it is the distance from Brahmarandhra at the top of the skull to Bhrumadhya. It is measured by following the curve of the head at the length of twelve fingers. This applies only to a yogi in the state of Samadhi.

The third is the supreme dvadasanta, or Sahasrara, known only by those who have identified with Shiva. Located at twelve fingers' breadth from Brahmarandhra, it is no longer connected with the physical body.

It is said that a yogi will live longer if the force of exhalation is less than the length of twelve fingers from the nose.

When breath remains inside the nostrils, it enables the practitioner to stay alive as long as he wishes. The description of that breath can be found in chapter 5 of *Bhagavad Gita*. This knowledge can be obtained only from the words of Guru.

गोरख उवाच

स्वामीजी! कौण सरोवर सनाल,
कोण मुखी बंचिवा जम का जाल।
लोक अगोचर कासों लहै,
मन पवना कैसे सम रहे॥

Gorakh says:

Swami ji! What is [this] pond,
Who is [in there] with a [lotus-like] stalk?
How [can] one save oneself from the net of Yam?*
How can one enjoy the invisible (*agochar*)?
How do mind and breath stay in equipoise?

---

* Yam is the Lord of Death in Hinduism.

श्री मच्छन्द्र उवाच

अवधू! मन सरोवर अंगुल बारा* बहे,
रोज करे जप थिरता गहे।
सहजे लोक अगोचर लहे,
मन पवना ऐसे सम रहे॥

Shri Machhendra says:

Avadhu! Mind flows like a lake [in the form
                                    of breath]
To the [distance of] twelve fingers.
Do repeat practice daily, tranquility will deepen.
One can enjoy the invisible spontaneously;
Thus mind and breath stay in balance.

᳘ Poetic comparisons help to deepen the understanding of mind-breath connection; accentuated metaphors of these words also spell a formula of immortality.

The flow of breath dissolves at the distance of twelve fingers from the nostrils, connecting mind-spirit to the outer void.

To the question "How [can] one save oneself from the net of Yam?" Machhendranath says, "Do repeat practice daily, tranquility will deepen."

---

* Shailendra Sharma considers that due to multiple re-writing of the original shloka from manuscript to manuscript, the Hindi word "baarah" (बारह, "twelve") was misspelled as "baaraa" (बारा, "big").

The state of mind is directly affected by the nature and intensity of airflow fed by breath. Fast breathing indicates turbulence of mind, slow and steady breath results in calmer senses and mental balance. Breath creates waves and ripples on the lake of mind or keeps the surface of its waters intact. The lotus of sleeping consciousness blossoms in the stillness of mind.

In Mohan Singh's book "Gorakhnath and Medieval Hindu Mysticism" we can find another variant of Guru Machhendra's answer, which is worth commenting upon:

Mind is a pond, breath (pavan) is one with a stalk (lotus).
By becoming upwards-faced (urdh mukhi)
One [can] ward off the Lord of Death –Yam.
[By knowing] lower and upper one [can] reach and enjoy
the Invisible.
Thus opinion gives Machendra. *

The seat of mind (the physical brain and cerebral fluid) is compared with a lake, while the stalk in it refers to the spinal cord attached to the skull. Breath travels up the spine, feeding the flower of mind.

When regular yogic sadhana forces the lotus of consciousness to bloom, the seeker becomes *urdh-mukhi*. Interestingly enough, the lotus bud is also called "urdh-mukhi," or "facing upwards."

Such a state is reached when the "mantra of breath" is practiced with rigorous dedication: the current of breath changes its direction by going upwards. This is a description of Prana entering Sushumna.

---

* मन सरोवर पवन सुनाला । उरध मुखि होई बंचीवा जम काल ।
अरध उरध अगोचर लवि लहै । ऐस वचार मछंदर कहै ।

The term "urdh-mukhi" is also used to delineate the mastery of celibacy, and with both components mentioned here, the net of Yam, Lord of Death, can be avoided; Kaal-Time can be warded off by the attained immortality.

But in this dialog two immortal yogis are not discussing the results of practice. They are conversing about the knowledge lying beyond it.

> *One can enjoy the invisible spontaneously;*
> *Thus mind and breath stay in balance*

Subconsciousness-Prana remains in upper centers and Apana, conscious mind, dwells in the lower "energy wheels." These are the basic pillars of life and existence.

Consciousness-Apana attracts and captures breath, the carrier of Prana, drawing it inside. Prana, or the subconscious, always remains hidden and internal.

Everything in this world is an expression of Greater Consciousness; by observing inner transformations, we can learn a great deal of its mechanism. The human body is the very expression of mind.

Let's say that the body is all-conscious Apana and hidden subconsciousness is Prana. Transforming conscious mind into the subconscious state, in yogic terms, signifies the state of suspended animation; united with Prana, Apana rests while subconsciousness prevails. Discover Prana – and the discovery of subconscious mind and its nature will follow, eventually unveiling super-mind.

Shiva Purana describes millions of years of elaborate and prolonged tapas, carried out by Shakti in hope to draw Shiva out of His Samadhi, to accept her and unite with her. This tapas still continues with every dedicated yogic practice and may bring indescribable effect of Supreme Unity: one can become fully established in the subconscious only by entering the state of suspended animation; then, in a breathless body, Prana awakens the subconscious mind.

Modern psychology states that although subconsciousness does not control the body, it has indirect but profound impact, affecting functions, reactions and processes in various and sometimes amazing ways.

All dormant possibilities waiting to be aroused, all vast lakes and oceans of memories and impressions lying in the subconsciousness are part of the omnipresent and omnipotent.

Spirit enters the body even when the subconscious mind is not awakened. Subconsciousness remains in the locked inner vault while spirit urges to reach for all treasures hidden there.

But when the body is dead and the spirit is gone, the treasure of subconsciousness will not be left behind.

Carrying its record, it travels with the spirit to its next destination, like a hidden gold coin sewn in the lining of the coat, still kept by the unaware carrier.

By controlling the flow of Prana and Apana and by replacing conscious mind with its subconscious "twin," the yogi merges with the invisible and unknowable, "Agochar."

The "unseen and unattainable" state of Agochar can be connected with Dhyan.

Commonly translated as "meditation," the real meaning of the Hindi word "dhyaan" differs from this interpretation.

In Hindi or Sanskrit an airplane is called "vayu-yaan," a spaceship is "antariksha-yaan," a ship is "jal-yaan" and a modern car is simply "yaan." "Yaan" is what carries, relocates and serves as a transporter.

When mind is placed in the carrier of intellect called "dhyaan," it is transported to the wisdom it is ready to face. Body does not change its position, but mind travels.

"Dhi" is super-intellect, and "yaan" is a vehicle or carrier: mind travels by the power of super-mind, transcendental intellect.

In addition to the act of sitting in meditation, "to sit in dhyaan" signifies the very fact of riding the chariot of the supreme intellect which carries the mind.

One can drive this chariot only by knowing the art of breath, skillfully holding its reins.

गोरख उवाच

स्वामीजी! कौण सविषमी करै संधि,
कौण चक्र लागे बंध।
कौण चेतन उनमुनि रहे,
सतगुरु होय सो पूछ्यां कहे॥

Gorakh says:

Swami ji! How can unevenness be balanced?
On which chakra should one put a lock (*bandh*)?
Which consciousness can stay transcendent
(*unmuni*)?
You are the true Guru, kindly answer the question.

─────────────── **50** ───────────────

श्री मच्छन्द्र उवाच

अवधू! अन विमली विषमी बंध,
चौकी ऊपर लागे बंध।
सदा चेतन उनमुन रहे,
ऐसा विचार मच्छन्द्र कहे॥

Shri Machhendra says:

Avadhu! Unevenness [can] be balanced
     by [applying] a few locks (*bandh*).
Apply a lock on the square (*chauki*).
Let consciousness always remain silent (*unmun*);
Thus opinion gives Machhendra.

ᴄᴜ Unevenness of Prana and Apana symbolizes permanent duality; breath purification fixes this imbalance.

Before moving to the second line of this shloka, let's ask ourselves: what do we know of Prana entering Sushumna and where exactly does it enter?

Flowing down from the heart, Prana enters Sushumna through Muladhara (where the tiny opening of Brahmadvaar lies at the end of the median channel) and strikes the earth element first.

In many graphic illustrations it is depicted as a golden square ("chauki") in Muladhara chakra. Invisible and unseen, Agochar Bandh (also known as Mulabandh) should be applied as a dam to redirect the flow of pranic energy into Brahmadvaar.

Mind is silenced as the energy of Kundalini Shakti, or the energy of Earth Itself, passes through all the remaining elements of higher chakras.

A new revision of the meaning of the key word "chauki" ("square") allows us to translate this shloka in a more laconic and direct way, redefining the key terms.

It is also worth commenting on the translation of another version of this shloka, which can be found in Dr. Mohan Singh's work.* It provides several interesting interpretations helping to understand the ultimate goals of yoga.

The Pure (anil) and the Stainless (vimal) are the difficult and easy forms of union (sandh).
The dam is to be applied above the chakki nerve center.
*The always-awake can attain to self-transcendence (unmuni)***

Anil is the Sun; Vimal is the Moon; synonymous with Apana and Prana, they also indicate the conscious and subconscious mind.

Just like planets, Sun and Moon, Apana and Prana are constantly on the move, being the reason for continuity of the flow of life itself.

Purification of body and mind with the following conversion into the stainless state (vimal) is considered to be first (and relatively easy) step on the path of yogic quest toward a much

---

* "Gorakhnath and Medieval Hindu Mysticism"

** अनलि विमलि विषम संधि।
चाकी उपर लागै बंध।
सदा चेतिनि मनि उनिमन रहै।

larger goal of the union with oneself through the connection of conscious mind with its subconscious twin.

The great Guru Machhendranath considers this task to be achievable.

The English translation of "anil" as "pure" is not quite correct, although purity is also part of this condition.

Anil is the purifying fire of yoga; as any flame requires oxygen, its fire will burn only in the presence of air element, Vayu.

Even an iron rod can be melted and molded only when fire is supported by oxygen – Vayu. Similarly, vital breath – pranayama – supports the flame of sadhana and makes it strong enough to purify the seeker.

Alliance with one's self may take place after elaborate steps of purification through breath have been taken.

To preserve the purity of merged conscious and subconscious mind while retaining one's individuality makes this form of union most difficult and challenging.

Perhaps the discrepancies in several re-written original manuscripts affected Mohan Singh's interpretation of the Hindi word "chakki" as "millstone, grinder" versus "chauki," or "square," given in other sources. However, this variant of translation holds deep significance.

The ancient form "chakki" is one and the same everywhere in the world: connected by an axis in the center, flat round millstones crush and grind grain in rotation. The translation implies that by holding together two polar sides of duality and crushing the grains of his own mind, the sadhak arrives at the state of Unmuni, or self-transcendence.

Poets also used the word "chakki" in a symbolic way: one millstone represents birth, the other – death; like grains, all living beings are endlessly crushed between them, becoming the flour of new life and death.

In Kriya Yoga, the term "dam," or "bandh," is used for the description of a certain technique which allows one to stop the continuous cycle of death and rebirth.

In higher kriyas, the flow of Prana and Apana (compared to the rotation of disks in windmills) are connected by the tongue raised in Khechari Mudra as the connecting axis. Simultaneously with Khechari Mudra, the sadhak performs special head movements which stimulate the brain during a continuously repeated rotation.

Continuous movements of Prana and Apana eventually form their union and grind the ignorance of mind; the flow of breath is balanced by the yogic technique of Nabhi Kriya.

With a certain mudra the sadhak applies a "dam" near Nabhi – the navel center (at the belly button, to be precise), where the flow of life – vital breath – rolls in and out. Nabhi is a lock or dam on the top of chakki nerve center.

Without a connecting center piece (tongue in Khechari Mudra) or without a dam (Nabhi Kriya), the windmill will not work and the grinding process will fail.

Once the great poet Kabir saw a grinder and started to cry. He understood the constant movement of life and death and their unbreakable connection: not a single grain, not a single creature would escape its fate, being caught between these two forces.

All grain on the periphery will be crushed between the stone discs, drawn to the edges by the power or inertia of rotation, death and rebirth.

However, some unprocessed grains will always remain closer to the center.

These yogis who stayed awake and remained "in the center" by entering the central channel of Sushumna will obtain the true knowledge and will be untouched by destruction and transformation.

Yogic practice grants permanent awakening and alertness: those with the sparkle of ultimate wisdom will move to the central axis, choosing the middle way to avoid duality, to remain in between of breaths in the endless union of conscious and subconscious.

The state of self-transcendence is achieved when the seeker has established himself in the state of subconsciousness and exited the boundaries of conscious, limited mind. Physical process (Khechari Mudra, Nabhi Kriya and other highly technical practices) will help the yogi to crush the grain of conscious mind and achieve Unmuni, the state of self-transcendence.

गोरख उवाच

स्वामीजी! कहां ते उत्पना व्यापक कहां,
आदि का स्तुति समाई।
ए तत गोसाई कहो समझाई,
जहां हमारी उत्पत्ति रहाई॥

Gorakh says:

Swami ji! Where is It [Omnipresent Origin]
born from?

Where does It spread?

Where does the praise of the Origin pervade?

You are the true Guru, kindly explain:

Where does [the source of] our origin remain?

---------------------- **52** ----------------------

श्री मच्छन्द्र उवाच

अवधू! तिल मध्ये यथा तेल,
काष्ठ मध्ये हुतासन ।
पहुप मध्ये यथा बास,
यूं देही में देवता ॥

Shri Machhendra says:

Avadhu! Like a sesame seed [contains] the same oil,
Like firewood [contains] fire,
Like a flower [contains] the same fragrance,
In the same way God [resides] in a mortal being.

◠ Yoga states that by realizing himself and recognizing his own origin, the seeker will realize all other things in creation. We are part of a larger world created from one single source: the recognition of one's individual source will lead to realization of the universal root of Creation.

The essence of a sesame seed, oil is already present in it before extraction. Fire already resides in the wood, waiting to be ignited. Fragrance lives in the petals of a flower as its essence. Spirit, the very pith of life, resides in the body, waiting to be discovered, longing to be befriended...

Ghee (melted butter) is always present in milk but never seen. Left without processing, milk will go sour and ghee will never get a chance to emerge. After heating the milk, cooling it down, converting it into curd and churning it, we'll receive butter;

one more heating – and ghee will appear. It is the immortal substance of milk.

Immortal substance lives in every human, waiting to be discovered, brought out, waiting to introduce itself. The power of tapas, knowledge of the goal and controlled will help to extract any essence out of its container.

But not so many people dare to get in touch with it and that's probably why the spirit keeps taking body after body, frustrated with the long waiting and loneliness.

Ways and methods of communication with one's own spirit are unknown to an ordinary body carrier; but yogis established long ago that it is possible to set up contact with Atma by controlling, guiding and managing breath.

Throughout the centuries people have held endless arguments and discussions about the origin of God, heaven, the nature of spirituality, parallel realms and dimensions, but the origin of the Creator of spirit remains the greatest of mysteries.

Yoga gives the most direct method of such a discovery, activating the real power of breath and its unseen substance, Prana, and honoring it as a connecting link between body and soul. The praise of Origin is the recognition of the nature of breath and its acceptance as the essence of Self.

Yoga directs the seeker to develop himself by controlling his breath, learning of its origin and then discovering his own Atma, or spirit.

Spirit knows its source and will share this mystery with a true seeker. That's why Matsyendranath says: "Let your spirit become your Guru, then your mind becomes a chela, disciple."

53

गोरख उवाच

स्वामीजी! श्रपणी कहौ कै कौणे भाई,
बंक नाल है कौणे ठाई।
जब यह प्राणि निशि करे,
पिंड मध्ये प्राण पुरुष कहां रहे॥

Gorakh says:

Swami ji! How is Snake-Kundalini (*shrapani*)
                              said to be attracted?
Where does bank naal dwell?
When a living being (*prani*) goes to sleep,
Where does Praan Purush,* manifested
                              in the body, reside?

---

* Praan Purush means jiva (soul), see also shloka 61 about jiva.

---- 54 ----

श्री मच्छन्द्र उवाच

अवधू! श्रपणी कहो के सहज सुभाई,
बंक नाल है नाभि ठाई ।
जब यह प्राण निशि करे,
पिंड मधि प्राण पुरुष अपरछंद रहे ॥

Shri Machhendra says:

Avadhu! Snake-Kundalini (*shrapani*) is said to
Be attracted [to Prana] spontaneously.
Navel is the place where bank naal dwells.
When this Prana goes to sleep,
Praan Purush, manifested in the body, stays
in aparchand [higher place].

In this shloka we read about powerful sublime experiences: Kundalini energy, moved by spontaneous attraction to Prana in the reactivated navel center, rises toward upper chakras. Prana will remain inside the physical body continuously and uninterrupted, providing an everlasting life of supreme consciousness.

But first let's establish the true meaning of some terms.

"Shrapani," or a "female snake," is a commonly known term for Kundalini Shakti. It is said to be "naturally attracted" to Prana-Shiva.

Puranas describe Adi Shakti's tapas which She performed for millions of years in hope to awake and attract Shiva. In a similar spontaneous and sudden wave of attraction, Shrapani (Kundalini-Shakti) moves towards Prana-Shiva that flows in through Nabhi (navel) – the life center. Only great tolerance allows a yogi to withstand the powerful current of the rising energy.

The umbilical cord, or "naal," which connects a fetus with the mother's body, turns into an inner root. Curved and archlike ("bank"), it is inside the embryo's navel.

Creation of the entire body starts form the life center (Nabhi), and the mechanism of life support keeps the future human safe till the moment of his emergence into the outer world. The child lives in the womb without breathing oxygen through the lungs: life force flows into his body through bank naal.

After the delivery the child's cord is cut off, and that simple operation turns off the initial mechanism of creation and transforms "in-the-womb Pranic breathing" into "outer-world intake of oxygen via lungs."

The direct meaning of the first part of this shloka can be summed up as: "When Shrapani-Kundalini feels spontaneous attraction towards Prana in the navel center, where bank naal is activated again via Nabhi Kriya, then Prana will remain inside the physical body uninterrupted."

Using the powers of Nabhi Kriya, the yogi turns on the unique intake of life-sustaining Prana through bank naal. The ability to switch on the mechanism of revitalization through the navel center starts the process of regeneration anew, and the yogi begins his travel toward immortality.

Gorakh repeats in his latest sayings ("padas"):

"The breath in front of the nose,
Ida and Pingala should be harmonized.
After 600 000 chants Anahat will rise effortlessly.
In the curved vein Sun will rise,
And from every pore the sound of trumpet will be heard."

Here again bank naal is translated into English as a "curved vein," but the true meaning of this obscure yogic term could be perceived only by initiated and practicing seekers with the help of a true Guru.

When this Prana goes to sleep,
Praan Purush, manifested in the body, stays in
aparchand [higher place]

Boundaries of the "domain" of Sahasrara chakra are measured from the tip of the tongue raised in Khechari Mudra.

It is a lotus with one thousand petals; its shining rays or spikes of the "wheel" bloom in "aparchand" ("up and above" – cranium and brain). In yogic terms, these lines speak about the activated crown chakra in the state of awakened consciousness.

It is up to Guru to see the depth of a disciple's question, and Matsyendranath answers very directly: Praan Purush, or vital breath, lives in aparchand (physiologically in the brain; by yogic criteria – in Sahasrara) while Prana in the heart center goes into suspended animation.

A continuous flow of vital breath (Prana) provides and guarantees life of the body. Expressed by the very fact of living and animating its carrier, life itself is just a shadow of Prana, which flows throughout the entire body, equally present and undivided in each and every cell.

In the heart center Prana* reaches its highest concentration: it nourishes heartbeats and supports the whole life system.

Prana in Hriday center "goes to sleep," and the yogi remains in suspended animation. At the same time transformed Prana unites with Apana and enters Sushumna, awakening Kundalini. Energy rises to the cranium, aparchand.

There Praan Purush (the true self, the soul animated by Prana) transforms mind into super-consciousness.

---

* Different types of Prana are described in numerous yogic texts. Simultaneous control of these Pranas should be mastered in the course of guided practice

गोरख उवाच

स्वामीजी! कौण चक्र में दिन करि चंद,
कौण चक्र में लागे बंध।
कौण चक्र में पवन निरोधे,
कौण चक्र में मन परमौधे।
कौण चक्र में धारे ध्यान,
कौण चक्र में लीजे विश्राम॥

Gorakh says:

Swami ji! In which chakra does Moon
create the day?

Upon which chakra should a lock (*bandh*)
be applied?

At which chakra should breath be held?

In which chakra does mind delight (*paramoudhe*)?

In which chakra should meditation (*dhyaan*)
be held?

At which chakra should one rest?

श्री मच्छन्द्र उवाच

अवधू! अर्ध चक्र में दिन करि चंद,
ऊर्ध चक्र में लागे बंध।
नाभी चक्र में पवन निरोधे,
हिरदा चक्र में मन परमौधे।
काष्ठ चक्र में धारे ध्यान,
ज्ञान चक्र में लीजे विश्राम॥

Shri Machhendra says:

Avadhu! In the middle (*ardh*) chakra Moon
creates the [new] day;
Apply a lock (*bandh*) upon the upper (*urdh*)
chakra.
Hold breath at the navel (*naabhi*) chakra;
Mind is delighted (*paramoudhe*) in the heart
chakra.
Hold meditation (*dhyaan*) in Kaashth chakra;*
Take rest in the chakra of wisdom (*gyaan chakra*).

In the middle (ardh) chakra Moon creates the [new] day

～ Both Muladhara and Swadhisthana centers are called
Ardh chakras. In these very centers the union of Prana and
Apana takes place and the ascent of Kundalini to the upper
chakras begins. Reaching Nabhi, the life power intake center in

---

* In Mohan Singh's work "Gorakhnath and Medieval Hindu Mysticism"
this chakra is called "Kaanth" chakra (the "throat" chakra).

the middle of the body, united Prana and Apana start the dawn of a new day, the transformation of mind.

Shastras name Agya chakra and Sahasrara chakra as "urdh" – upper, higher chakras. Moon, or the mind, reaches its stable condition upon entering these centers via breath control.

Medulla oblongata (also called Agya chakra) is located in the lower back part of the brain. It controls the flow of breath.

In the higher (Agya or urdh) chakra, crescent moon appears as the symbol of a new day. Transformation of subconsciousness into consciousness is compared with the beginning of a new day for the mind: the night of ignorance is over and a powerful comprehension of reality is awakened.

Apply a lock (bandh) upon the upper (urdh) chakra

Jalandhar Bandh takes place in the upper chakra.

Myriads of primary and secondary nerve channels, or nadis, pass through the throat center: there main channels form a dense junction, running from the brain via the throat.

Yoga places a great importance on Jalandhar Bandh, calling it the "throat lock." By focusing attention on the throat center and gaining control over it, the practitioner eventually will gain command of all other chakras.

Hold breath at the navel (naabhi) chakra; Hold meditation (dhyaan) in Kaashth chakra

Here Nabhi center (navel point chakra) actually indicates the heart center, Hriday, where life force is concentrated.

Both Prana and mind should be taken to the void of the heart center; the seeker is instructed to focus upon it in meditation (or "hold dhyan in his heart").

This line contains highly technical details: in the state of suspended animation the yogi is instructed to "hold dhyan in Kaashth chakra." Kaashth chakra is a description of a state rather than an indication of an actual center: in suspended animation body becomes motionless and unresponsive – wood-like ("kaashth").

Concentrated in Hriday, mind obtains gyan, or true wisdom; the light of God will shine, and the seeker will take refuge in it.

Mind is delighted (paramoudhe) in the heart chakra

"Paramoudhe" is joy, and joy always flows from the heart. The basis of genuine joy is true knowledge.

Translated as "delight," "paramoudhe" is joy of the true gyan, confirmed to the mind by the knowing heart.

Take rest in the chakra of wisdom (gyaan chakra)

After Kundalini has risen and reached medulla oblongata, it takes rest in Agya chakra.

Some tantric Upanishads describe this center as the cradle of Bindu. Anatomically speaking, it is a junction where the spinal cord is attached to the brain.

In a properly executed Khechari Mudra the tongue is firmly installed in the cavity behind the upper palate; this passage is called "tallu." It opens access to Sahasrara chakra, serving as an inner gate to the higher center.

In fact, medulla oblongata, or Agya chakra, is located closer to Sahasrara than Bhrumadhya, the center between the eyes.

But the tongue raised in Khechari Mudra acts as a connecting link or extended bridge ("setu") for the flow of energy further, from Bhrumadhya up to Sahasrara. The naturally occurring in-between state of natural breathlessness, one of several conditions of coming closer to the state of Samadhi, is also called "setu."

The sadhak wins the right to rest only when his Kundalini has reached Agya chakra and taken refuge there. When the practitioner attains the state of immortality, all his mundane worries also come to rest and cease.

गोरख उवाच

स्वामीजी! कौण उदै माया शुनि,
नवग्रह कैसे पाप सु पुनि।
कौण ग्रह ले उनमुनि रहै,
सतगुरु होय सो पूछ्यां कहै॥

Gorakh says:

Swami ji! How does the void of illusion appear?
How can nine planets be good or bad?
With which planetary position [in horoscope]
can one
Achieve the state of transcendence (*unmuni*)?
You are the true Guru, kindly answer the question.

─── **58** ───

श्री मच्छन्द्र उवाच

अवधू! बोलत जैसे माया शुनि,
नवग्रह विचारे तो पाप न पुनि।
शिव शक्ति ले उनमुनि रहे,
ऐसा विचार मच्छन्द्र कहै॥

Shri Machhendra says:

Avadhu! The void of illusion is like speech.
If one considers [the position of] nine planets,
Then there is neither bad nor good.
With [the help of] Shiva and Shakti
One can attain the state of transcendence.
Thus opinion gives Machhendra.

☙ Minds of those who do not possess the knowledge of True Reality are clouded by illusion.

Illusion begins from speech, when a formless thought attempts to take shape through spoken word. The listener attaches his own imagery and perception of truth to the words spoken by another person. The speaker's words, in turn, bear the limitations of his individuality. Levels of mental development and comprehensive abilities are always mismatched, and that's why speech is considered as the lowest form of communication. It adds yet another thread of illusion to the all-pervading Maya. Mind-to-mind communication is the one and only true form of interaction in the void of deceptive reality.

Maya starts to disappear with the word of Guru, who instructs the sadhak to recognize the word of Naad.

After that the practitioner enters the state of *para-vani* – the divine vision, or direct mind-to-mind communication.

The usage of words is then no longer required; sounds of speech, hand gestures or eye movements lose their effectiveness. Speech is given up when the practitioner communicates with the Supreme Sound, divine word; illusion remains no longer.

At that level the yogi has already risen above all concepts of good and evil, perceiving them only as a play of consciousness, different expressions of One. He is no longer concerned about karmic effects.

Matsyendranath states that nine planets do not establish good or bad karmas, they are just astral indicators of all present potential and possibilities extracted from the summary of previous deeds. They give a blueprint of karmas, a road map or "travel guide" of a destiny, indicating past deeds and probable future results. Planets are merely objective indicators – traffic lights on the highway of one's fate.

If the yogi realizes the inner flow of Prana (Shiva) and Apana (Shakti), he will attain immortality and will enter the state of Unmuni.

In *Yoga Vasishtha* the immortal crow Kag Bhushundi explains to Rishi Vashishtha the roots of his ageless existence: "I became immortal by knowing the essence of Prana and Apana..."

59/MSP

गोरख उवाच

स्वामीजी! कुण उदै नग्र मंडली,
कुण ग्रसै हरि ब्रह्म का गुरु ।
विसरि जाउ तो कैसे तिरु ॥

Gorakh says:

Swami ji! How does a fellowship (*mandli*) arise
[inside] the city?
How can Hari [spirit], Guru of Brahm [mind],
be comprehended?
If I forget [the way], then how can I cross over?*

How does a fellowship (mandli) arise [inside] the city?

ᘐ Prana and Apana continuously circulate within the walls of the nine-gated city of body, keeping it alive. "Mandli" is the association of mind and spirit, of Guru and disciple; an association which arises within the city of body.

How can Hari [spirit], Guru of Brahm [mind], be comprehended?

Inside the town of the body, there is a fort of the heart inhibited by the immortal spirit – Atma, addressed as Hari.

---

* A slightly different translation of this shloka is given in Dr. Mohan Singh's "Gorakhnath and Medieval Hindu Mysticism":

"Which is the garden, the town and the mandal? In which city is the Guru? If I forget it, how am I to cross over [the ocean of Samsara]?"

Ancient yogis sang: "Hari Hari sumiran karo!" – "Remember Hari!" With time, this transformed into a religious accost, one of the many names of Krishna and Vishnu. The literal meaning of "Hari" ("haran karnevala") is "the one who takes away." Atma's power to grant life to a body also signifies the ability to take life at will; that's why yogis called spirit-Atma *Hari*, or the "stealer of life."

Mind-Brahm (not Brahma) resides in the body, the city with nine gates. Within the walls of the body, Hari-spirit becomes the Guru of Brahm-mind. When it happens, they form a great bondage and never leave the city of the body.

In these plain words Guru Matsyendranath gives a formula for immortality.

If I forget [the way], then how can I cross over?

Gorakhnath asks: If I forget (about the union of mind and spirit) and lose the way, then how can I cross the ocean of consciousness?*

---

* None of the available manuscripts offer a shloka with Matsyendranath's answer to this specific question, but several explanations on the subject of mind-spirit union are embedded in the body of the dialog.

60

गोरख उवाच

स्वामीजी! कौणे घर कौणे बास,
कौणे गर्भ रह्या दश मास।
कौण मुखि पाणी कौण मुखिता खीर,
कौण दिशा उत्पति भया शरीर॥

Gorakh says:

Swami ji! Which is the house, who dwells [in it]?

Who stays in the womb for ten months?

Through which mouth does [he] take water?
How does [he] take food?

In which direction is the formed body born?

61

श्री मच्छन्द्र उवाच

अवधू! अनिलु आतम बास,
आया गर्भ रह्या दश मास ।
नाभि कंवल मुखि पाणी खीर,
वायुकार शनतपति भया शरीर ॥

Shri Machhendra says:

Avadhu! Air is the house of the spirit;
[He] comes into a womb and stays
for ten [lunar] months.
Through the navel [cord which is] like
a [stem of] lotus [he] takes water and food.
The formed body makes a transfer
to the domain of air.

Air is the house of the spirit

∾ Formless Void is the house of the spirit, and unconditioned mind is the one who knows, who is aware ("avagati").
Unconditioned consciousness is the one who knows the house,
who is able to comprehend his habitation – the house of Great
Emptiness. And that's where Consciousness of the Void resides.

[He] comes into a womb and stays for ten [lunar] months

"He" is jiva, the identity of an individual soul. Yogic texts mostly
refer to jiva as "he." During Samadhi jiva resides in Atit Shunya –
the Supreme Void.

After ten lunar months of continuous state of Samadhi, Jiva unites with Atma, becoming Jivatma. In other words, the unification of Shiva and Shakti takes place.

Through the navel [cord which is] like a [stem of] lotus [he] takes water and food

This part of dialog refers to Nabhi Kriya as well as to Khechari Mudra: the sadhak activates the power of intake of Prana through the navel while keeping Khechari. When tongue is inserted behind the upper palate, mouth becomes watered. This is "water from the inner well." Prolonged practice of Khechari Mudra in combination with other special techniques stimulates brain centers; certain hormonal fluid is formed and "milked out." Khechari activates the inner "mouth" – the cavity where the erected tongue is placed; from there Amrita (the elixir of immortality) flows.

The formed body makes a transfer to the domain of air

Spirit comes from the astral world to take the shape of a body, to develop conscious mind and travels back to the formless when the life of the physical body is over.

The child appears in the domain of air the very moment he starts to breathe through the nose. Only in the domain of air, by the grace of his guru, the disciple starts to master breathing through pranayama and the art of yoga using air (pavan), and his journey towards Omkar begins.

"Omkar" is commonly connected with the sound of "Om," yet its meaning, according to the Sanskrit dictionary, is different: "sthanantakaran" or "sthanapati" means "transference from one place to another."

Ultimately everyone who enters this world in the vessel of physical body is born in the direction of Omkar.

The appearance of jiva and the following transfer of consciousness from the womb into the mundane world is Omkar.

Spirit departs from the body upon completion of physical life and transits to the astral dimension, towards Omkar.

Journey from the most secure place (mother's womb) takes a new spirit to the most unpredictable place (earthly realm), and when the life of the physical carrier is over, Omkar, or transfer to yet another, different realm, happens again.

गोरख उवाच

स्वामीजी! कौण नाली होय शिव संचरया,
कौण मुख पैठा जीव ।
कौण गर्भ वसंतड़ा,
कौण नाली रस पीव ॥

Gorakh says:

Swami ji! Through which channel (*naali*)
is Shiva moved?

Where does the soul (*jiv*) sit?

Who inhabits the womb?

Through which channel (*naali*) does [he] drink
the elixir (*ras*)?

श्री मच्छन्द्र उवाच

अवधू! संखणी नाली होय शिव संचरया,
सुषुमणि पैठा जीव ।
माया गर्भ वसंतड़ा,
बंकनाल रस पीव ॥

Shri Machhendra says:

Avadhu! Shiva is moved through Shankhini naali.
The soul resides in Sushumna.
[He] resides in the womb of Maya and
Drinks the elixir (*ras*) through bank naal.

Through which channel (naali) is Shiva moved? – Shiva is moved through Shankhini naali

∽ Some translators mistakenly decrypt this process as *vajroli*, interpreting "Shiva" as "seminal liquid." But this shloka has a different meaning, describing the most secretive of yogic techniques. 72 000 nadis are subtle currents of vital energy, or Prana Shakti, which emanates from chakras and spreads throughout the entire body. The most important nadis are Ida, Pingala and Sushumna, or the median channel ("madhya nadi"). Along this nadi, which is as delicate as lotus fiber, Prana and Kundalini ascend to the summit. Being empty, Sushumna offers no obstruction: only in its void the breath vibrates and becomes conscious again, recovering its universal essence. Chakras are situated along this median channel; rising Kundalini pierces them one by one during her ascent. Formed in the subtle body with prolonged and fierce practice of yoga, these centers do not belong to the gross physical body, although their development starts in the cerebral fluid of the spinal cord.

An ordinary man does not even have formed chakras, they exist as rudimentary "entangled knots" (granthi), "clogging" jiva and strengthening the sense of ego.

The pathway of breath is called "Shankhini": drawn schematically, it resembles the silhouette of a conch shell – "shankha" in Sanskrit. From the heart center Prana-Shiva follows this trajectory and comes down to Muladhara chakra. United with Apana, Prana enters Sushumna through the opening at the end of the middle channel called Brahmadvaar.

Awakened by united Prana-Apana, Kundalini rises up the Sushumna, piercing other chakras along its path and reaches Agya chakra (or physical brain), where a special reaction takes place, stimulating the flow of "nectar," or "elixir," into the cavity of the upper throat. In there, secreted by the brain, the precious mysterious elixir Amrita will be received by the sadhak's raised tongue during Khechari Mudra.

[He] resides in the womb of Maya and drinks the elixir (ras) through bank naal

In the womb an embryo's development starts from the navel center, which connects it to the mother's body via the umbilical cord ("naal"). The inner portion of its root inside the fetus body, curved and tilted, is called "bank naal" – the mysterious center of creation, which triggers the development of the entire body.

When a child is born, the cord is cut off, and that turns off the initial mechanism of creation. If someone is able to activate this mechanism again by switching it on, then the process of rejuvenation of the body will continue. That's why Naabhi Kriya technique is considered one of the most powerful tools of Kriya Yoga. The yogi who is able to switch on revitalization through the navel center is compared to an embryo undergoing the process of full development before emerging out of the womb into the world.

A siddha who drinks Prana through bank naal is considered to be still living in his mother's womb: his body continuously regenerates, upgrades and sustains itself in the everlasting form.

गोरख उवाच

स्वामीजी! कौण शून्य उत्पन्ना आई,
कौण शुनि सतगुरु सु बुझाई ।
कौण शुनि में रह्या समाय,
ए तत गुरु कहो समझाय ॥

Gorakh says:

Swami ji! In what void is [he] born?

Which void is explained [to him] well
by the true Guru (*satguru*)?

In what void does [he] stay absorbed?

O Guru, kindly explain that essence (*tat*).

65

श्री मच्छन्द्र उवाच

अवधू! सहज उत्पन्न आई,
समि सुरत सतगुरु सु बुझाई।
अतीत शुनि में रह्या समाय,
परम तत कहूँ समझाय ॥

Shri Machhendra says:

Avadhu! [He] comes [to the void]
spontaneously (*sahaj*).
Concsiousness [of the void] of nearness (*sami surat*) is explained well by the true Guru.
[He] is absorbed in the void of past (*atit shuni*).
I explain [thus] the Supreme Tattva.*

〜 Here Matsyendranath names different stages of spontaneous fusion of individual mind with the Void.

In the very beginning of this journey, Satguru teaches his disciple to follow the sound of Naad, to observe the flow of Prana and to discover inner emptiness of his own body. Void carries all Matter, its particles and atoms. We are Void, It infills all cells of our bodies.

Having materialized out of emptiness, into the emptiness we shall depart. Being quite in tune with the biblical interpretation of the origin of all things, this statement reflects yogic views on Creation.

---

* The Supreme Tattva ("essence") is Time, which resides in all voids.

The practitioner becomes aware of it, understanding that all earthlings came out of Void and took different shapes in these physical bodies, carriers of emptiness, as 99.9% of flesh tissue, its cells and molecules consists of Shunya (Void).

Without directions from a true Teacher, it is nearly impossible to fully comprehend yourself as a child of Emptiness and carrier of the Void. This discovery happens through guided breath practice: a seeker is taught to identify himself with his breath, as it signifies attachment to life.

The yogi realizes that his flesh is a vessel of Prana: it flows from the outer Greater Void and infills the shunya of his body.

Then he starts to understand that his own essence IS conscious Prana, who, together with Sound, acts as a link between him and the Source of his own origin, Void.

Again and again breath infills the cavities of his bodily shell and leaves it with each exhalation, conforming this connection.

The void of nearness (Samip Shunya) – the space outside the husk of the body – starts at the point where breath dissolves.

Following his own breath, the yogi spontaneously merges with the outer void.

New self-identification comes when he recognizes himself as part of the outer Emptiness. For him Duality ceases, as he is no more deceived by the "separateness" from the Whole.

Subtle metaphysical transformations of mind and the sound of Naad trigger spontaneous recollection of past as the yogi enters Atit Shunya,* the void of unattachment.

---

* See shlokas 73 and 123, explaining a wider meaning of Atit.

"Atit" is past, and past is the origin of everything presently existing. The root of past is planted in Time merged within Void along with the mystery of all previous births and reasons for the present existence.

Awakened subconsciousness absorbs into past and sees its root. The sadhak recognizes memories of his previous births and understands his past karmas. Then his mind "voids" them by detaching from the past forever.

Climax comes as the full merger of an individual mind with the conscious Void, where it stays forever.

Consecutive steps are: understanding of one's own emptiness, identification with one's own breath and universal Prana, recognition of Greater Emptiness when the breath of an individual breather disappears in the outer space. Recognition of one's personal history grants freedom and cuts ties as the Sound and vibration of Naad lead the sadhak into the Great Void.

Param Tattva, or the Highest Tattva, the Supreme Time, opens to the yogi after he has traveled through these experiences.

The first glimpses of Truth come to him in the words of a human guru, who teaches him to hear the Sound, and then the Word of the Highest Guru, Time, enters his being in the supremacy of Anahat Naad.

The mission of an earthly Satguru is to guide his disciple to the Greater Conscious Void (Param Shunya) and to explain Its supreme essence (tattva) to the true seeker.

Shunya is all-pervading and conscious Shakti; every movement in the universe is possible only because of this great conscious emptiness.

Such qualities as stability and equipoise could be attributed only to the almighty Void; nothing existing within It can be called truly stabilized.

It is believed that every spirit, every soul is born from the formless and all-pervading space and carries qualities of its birthplace. That's why everyone who is craving to get "back home" can recognize the root of their own origin in the Void and Its Greater mind, which gave birth to this material World, including us.

When the seeker begins to understand Greater Consciousness and merges with It, his mind obtains the initial qualities of stability and equipoise. These are original properties of the Void – the origin and source of individual mind. This signifies the expiry of duality in the yogi's mind.

Passing through Emptiness, he discovers the Consciousness of Time waiting for him beyond the Void.

66

गोरख उवाच

स्वामीजी! कौण मुख लागे समाधि,
कोण मुख छूटे उपाधि।
कोण मुख जु तुरिया बंध,
कौण मुख अजरावर कंध॥

Gorakh says:

Swami ji! How can one attain Samadhi?
How can deception (*upaadhi*) disappear?
How can Turiya Bandh be achieved?
How can one make the body ever young?

--- **67** ---

श्री मच्छन्द्र उवाच

अवधू! मन सुखी वाला लागे समाधि,
पवन मुख बाला छूटे उपाधि।
सुरति मुख बाला तुरिया बंध,
गुरु मुख बाला अजरावर कंध॥

Shri Machhendra says:

Avadhu! The one whose mind is happy [can]
attain Samadhi.
Seeker (*baala*), deception (*upaadhi*) disappears
through breath.
Child (*baala*), Turiya Bandh is achieved
through contemplation (*surati*).
Child, an ever young body is attained
by Guru's words.

ᕱᕦ Translated as "young man" in "Gorakhnath and Medieval Hindu Mysticism," the term "bala" does not imply the actual age of the addressed person. There were times when Indian sadhus would address even an old man searching for the knowledge as "baccha" ("child"). Every novice taking his first steps on the path to knowledge is considered to be a child.

Disturbing factors ("upaadhi") on the way to the fourth state, Turiya, are frames of conditioned thinking: "I am a man," "I am a student," "I am an Indian," limiting one's actual self.

Attentive contemplation ("surati") is the initial concept and clause for the development of consciousness; it grants connection with the eternal and omnipresent sound, Anahat Naad, or Shabd.

At first, when attention, or contemplation, is not connected to Shabd, mind is asleep and inert. Real Gyan, knowledge and wisdom, enter the seeker's mind when the eternal Word, or the Sound, is heard.

Attention is no longer present in this state; it already brought mind to its destination, and mind enters a dream-like state, Turiya. Attention goes to sleep and the development of a super-conscious mind takes place.

Only through mind the seeker can enter the state of Samadhi and open new, different vistas. Satguru's guidance is a necessary provision for this quest.

By obeying the teaching and being attentive, the practitioner will deserve to be visited by Gyan, or higher knowledge. This will be the knowledge of the fact that everything in this world (including the seeker) consists of uncountable condensed expressions of the formless Void. With this realization all upadhis (deceptions), mistaken thoughts or disturbances of mind will disappear.

He will understand that the vast varieties of countless caused forms, states and expressions were created just for the sake of Divine play by great formless powers which exist in Infinity.

In order to travel through the perpetuity of time, the game of life and death, good and evil, night and day, the hero and the villain was invented; roles keep changing and shifting, and the play continues forever... The wise ones called this play *Lila*, or divine and endless entertainment.

Cleansed by pranayama and guided by a Satguru, a pure mind allows the seeker to enter the state of Samadhi. Under his Teacher's guidance and through his own tamed vital breath, the seeker will acquire the fourth state, Turiya.

Described in almost every yogic text, the fourth state lies beyond awakening, sleeping and dreaming. After a mind has reached and experienced Samadhi, it will be focused on recent experiences and will attempt to analyze them. That focus is called Turiya.

Entrance to the fourth state may be granted only after suspended animation has been achieved: it's impossible to enter Turiya without experiencing Samadhi first.

When mind emerges from the depths of Samadhi, it is filled with recognition of recent experience; and only then the yogi is able to acknowledge the fourth state.

The mind will continue to analyze this experience, appraising the new knowledge and wondering about further development.

No longer an ordinary intellect, the post-Samadhi mind will be able to comprehend this amazing experience and reach the conclusion about its results.

There is a good example given in many books: a virgin who has attended several childbirths will never experience labour pains, unless she becomes a mother herself. In the same way a pre-Samadhi mind will never achieve the depths of post-Samadhi consciousness.

The commentary on *Shiva Sutra* give a slightly different description of the fourth state.

In the beginning the experience of Samadhi appears like a dream to a sleeping mind, because an ordinary mind is permanently asleep. Very hard practice of yoga awakens the mind, and it experiences Samadhi: by realizing a dream which first appears dream-like, the yogi will reach the fourth state. Realization of the never-ending Life will enter and disperse through his entire being.

68

गोरख उवाच

स्वामीजी! कौण सोवे कौण जागे,
कौण दशूं दिश धावे।
कहां ते उठत पवना,
कवन कंठ तालिका बजावे॥

Gorakh says:

Swami ji! Who sleeps, who is awake?
Who runs in ten directions?
Where does breath (*pavan*) arise from?
How does the throat clap?

69

श्री मच्छन्द्र उवाच

अवधू! मन सोवे पवन जागे,
कल्याण दशूं दिशि धावे।
नाभि ते उठत पवना,
हौठ कण्ठ तालिका बजावे॥

Shri Machhendra says:

Avadhu! Mind goes to sleep; breath [air] is awake.
Happiness and grace (*kalyaan*) run in ten
                                                                    directions.
From the navel arises breath.
The throat claps through lips [producing voice].

∾ Nine gates in the "city" of the body receive grace from mind through the power of yogic tapas; with its "blessing" the seeker will gain access to the tenth gate, Brahmarandhra. Breath remains awakened while mind goes to sleep; consciousness becomes unconscious and observes itself in its sleep.

From Muladhara Prana enters the median channel and continues its journey to Nabhi; from there it ascends to Agya chakra. During its rise the grace (vital force of Prana) flows in all ten directions, towards all gates of the body.

Meanwhile, Khechari Mudra will have its effect on breath: a purified flow of air, passing through the soft upper palate, throat and lips, will produce a different and unique sound – the voice of the awakening spirit.

───────── **70** ─────────

गोरख उवाच

स्वामीजी! कहां ते करे मन गुण घणा,
कहां ते मन करे आवागवणा।
कौण मुख चांदना कर करै,
का मुख काल निद्रा करे॥

Gorakh says:

Swami ji! Where does mind acquire
many virtues from?
Where does mind come from and where
does it go to?
Who can face the rays of the [crescent] moon?
Where does Death sleep?

श्री मच्छन्द्र उवाच

अवधू! हृदय ते करे मन गुण घणा,
नाभी ते पवन करे आवा गवणा ।
आप मुख चांदना कर करै,
मन मुख काल निद्रा करे ॥

Shri Machhendra says:

Avadhu! Mind acquires many virtues
                    from the heart;
Breath comes from and goes to the navel.
[When] you [your mind] face[s] the rays
                    of the [crescent] moon,
Death (*kaal*) will sleep in the mouth of mind.

෴ Gorakh asks about the origin of mind, and his Guru gives
an answer on breath arising from the navel. Once again we are
told that consciousness is directly linked to Prana and vital
breath.

The true beauty of this earthly body is in the presence of the
spirit which dwells inside it. Known as Vasudev, or Time Itself,
the spirit lives in the human heart. Upon entering the heart it
unites with the essence of all, the Time, and acquires the virtues
of Its grace.

Understanding and attention flow from consciousness; the
fountain of nectar springs from mind itself. The flow of nectar
puts death to sleep, and life remains awakened forever.

Crescent moon denotes immortality. The yogi realizes the power of Prana and identifies with each inhalation flowing into his body and each exhalation which slips into the outer void. His mind becomes powerful and limitless, traveling beyond his physical shell, and he overcomes time and death.

गोरख उवाच

स्वामीजी! कौन ज्योति ते पवना पलटे,
कौन शून्य ते वाचा फुरे।
कौन शून्य ते त्रिभुवन सार,
कौन शुनि ते उतरिया पार॥

Gorakh says:

Swami ji! Which light does breath (*pavan*)
reverse from?
Which void does speech arise from?
Which void does the essence of
three worlds [come] from?
Through which void can one go [beyond]
to the other side?

———————————— 73 ————————————

श्री मच्छन्द्र उवाच

अवधू! उग्र शून्य ते ज्योति पलटे,
अभय शून्य ते बाचा फुरे ।
परम शून्य ते त्रिभुवन सार,
अतीत शून्य उतरिया पार ॥

Shri Machhendra says:

Avadhu! From furious void (*ugra shunya*)
                        light reverses.
From fearless void (*abhai shunya*) speech arises.
The essence of three worlds [comes] from
                the Supreme Void (*param shunya*).
The void of the past (*atit shunya*) takes
                [one beyond] to the other side.

〜 Void is one, Its expressions are numerous. Creation or annihilation of the universe aggravates Void, giving birth to the fire of destruction or light of creation, in which the ever-pervading breath of universal Prana reverses (starts emanating) at the point of its own origin.

Evolution of initial elements begins as condensation and compression of universal Emptiness, inherent to the space at the time of turbulent transformations.

First, born out of vibration of the Void, appears Akash-ether. Being almost a reflection of formless Shunya, it carries the ability to condense and transform, which will be escalated in the chain of future metamorphoses. When ether becomes "rageful," stirred in the turbulence of aggravated Void, it condenses and becomes air. The element of Vayu-air carries in itself properties of the fire element, such as dryness and combustion. Transformed in excitation, air becomes fire.

Out of condensed Agni-fire comes the "liquid flame" of water, which, in turn, manifests itself as the element of earth. Every particle and atom carries a seed of ebullience and fire waiting for incitation.

Breath reverses at the point of emanation, at its own source. To find the point of its origin, breath (Apana, or conscious mind) will have to travel against breath (Prana, or subconscious mind), like a surfer travels over the surf.

Reversed to find its own undivided source, conscious mind keeps traveling in order to merge with its subconscious twin at the point of origin, where both of them can exist in unity.

In the fire of yogic practice, Prana and Apana reverse their flow and merge together in the void of the median channel, Sushumna. And that is how the dance of energy, Tandava of Kundalini, begins.

Here the word "shunya" has a symbolic meaning, describing a state significant for such a journey: the goal will not be reached without a strong determination, and there is no victory without eagerness to learn. It is the starting point of many discoveries.

The light of mind is eager to study itself; the mind always inquires about the mystery of its own birth; this inquiry leads it back to the mindless state with the help of reversed breath.

From fearless void (abhai shunya) speech arises

Speech arises from the Consciousness of the Void, where an ordinary fear remains no longer.

The yogi, being present in the Void, has already gone beyond all fears of mundane world, leaving them where such emotions belong.

The fear of death is the basis of all fears. An adept becomes aware of the Conscious Void by completing his journey beyond the limits of his own physical existence. He arrives there when his own consciousness has been developed to the level where physical limitations no longer exist. Fear does not reach beyond the limits of physicality.

The essence of three worlds [comes] from the Supreme Void (param shunya)

Bhur, Bhuvar and Svaha are three worlds called *vyaahritis*, or fields of experience for souls. Bhur is the physical (or gross, earthly) plane, Bhuvar is a more subtle world closely connected to the earthly realm but constituted of finer matter; Svaha is the causal world.

These worlds can be subjectively associated with the dream-like state, awakened state and a deep state of consciousness.

Void, or Shakti, holds the essence of all the three worlds. Consider Shakti as a synonym of the Void, a mighty power and a reason for the absence of fear in Its domain.

The ability to control all three worlds arises from Shunya.

The importance of self-mastery is stressed as the first step towards recognition of the greater Void: Its understanding comes only after a yogi has realized the nature of his own inner void.

Shunya of the heart is the key to existence of life in the body. This void has to be explored, understood and realized by the practitioner via mastery of breath.

Upon realizing the essence and nature of the inner void of the heart, the yogi will understand the roots of Atma, or Self, and the reasons behind his own existence.

Then the seeker will progress further, first discovering the Greater Void and hereafter sensing and attempting to understand the Void's Consciousness.

By mastering Self (by realizing one's own inner void) one achieves recognition of Param Shunya, the holder of all three realms.

In later poetry Gorakh defines controlled mind as a key to three planes of reality:

This very Mind is Shakti, this very mind is Shiva.
This very mind is the life of five elements.
The one who controls mind and remains in what is beyond mind,
He may speak about secrets of the three worlds.

Gorakh Bani ("The Sayings of Gorakh") (50)

The void of the past (atit shunya) takes [one beyond] to the other side

By detaching from the past which clouds his concentration, by disconnecting every tie with material and mundane existence, the yogi plants himself into the depth of the Void.

From the yogic point of view it can be illustrated with the following example.

The state of suspended animation is the one and only true certification that consciousness has entirely detached itself from all five elements, departed the bodily plane and entered the Void, or merged with Shakti.

When mind travels to its very core the adept develops a new level of consciousness.

The state of Samadhi is considered to be the highest level of yogic achievement and is measured by one single criterion: real detachment from senses and objects, emotions and their ruling forces, gunas, takes place only in suspended animation. In Samadhi mind resides in the Void, merged with Shakti.

All life processes slow down or shut without permanent termination; all links to the outer world are cut, and the mind breaks out of its cage, flowing freely into the Void.

There the adept becomes conscious of super-consciousness – Paramhans, the Great Swan.

Such are the highest results of yogic practice.

No devotion or righteous living can grant the same level of understanding and realization. Attention will be diverted to small mundane things, a bigger picture of life will be ever-evasive, and the Highest Reality will remain inaccessible.

गोरख उवाच

स्वामीजी! कहां ते उत्पन्नी बुध्या,
कहां ते उत्पन्ना अहार ।
कहां ते उत्पन्नी निद्रा,
कहां ते उत्पन्ना काल ॥

Gorakh says:

Swami ji! Where does intellect arise from?
Where does food appear from?
Where does sleep emerge from?
Where does Death (*kaal*) originate from?

———————————— 75 ————————————

श्री मच्छन्द्र उवाच

अवधू! मनसा ते उत्पन्नी बुध्या,
बुध्या ते उत्पन्ना अहार।
अहार ते उत्पन्नी निद्रा,
निद्रा ते उत्पन्ना काल ॥

Shri Machhendra says:

Avadhu! Intellect arises from mind.
Food appears from intellect.
From food emerges sleep.
Out of sleep originates Death.

〜 Intellect emerges from mind in search of knowledge; hunger instigates search for provision, hungry mind demands food in the form of Gyan.

Even search for real food starts from the intellectual ability to register this urge. Desire always lies at the root of any hunger; it triggers the initial wish for different types of fulfillment.

Appease a certain hungry desire with the very food it craves, fulfil its cravings and thirst, and eventually the satisfied yearning will fall asleep, entering a state of "little death," as sleep is called sometimes.

"Chewing" upon ideas, ultimately mind goes to sleep; sleep comes from mind – its exhaustion or satisfaction.

Upon fulfilling a hungry desire one should move away from it without waking it up. Move on to meet another hunger, appease it and keep moving on until finally no unsatisfied desires remain.

Feeding hunger allows to expose its roots and to see things from different angles: one will discover that the stomach doesn't care about the actual taste of food and that taste buds belong to the tongue.

The highest satisfaction comes to mind when the urge to solve the mystery of its own origin is finally satisfied.

गोरख उवाच

स्वामीजी! कौण कंवल हम सास उसास।
कौण कंवल हम हंसा वास।
कौण कवल हम पूजा करां।
कौण कवल हम अलख कौ ग्रहां॥

Gorakh says:

Swami ji! At which lotus should I inhale
and exhale?

At which lotus should I settle [my] swan (*hansa*)?

At what lotus should I perform worship (*puja*)?

At what lotus should I comprehend
the invisible (*alakh*)?

श्री मच्छन्द्र उवाच

अवधू! नाभ कवल तुम सास उसासै।
हिरदा कवल तुम हंसा बासै।
मधि कंवल तुम पूजा करौ।
अचिंत कवल तुम अलख कौ ग्रहौ॥

Shri Machhendra says:

Avadhu! Inhale and exhale at the navel lotus.
Settle [your] swan at the heart lotus.
Perform worship (*puja*) at the central lotus.
Comprehend the invisible (*alakh*) at the lotus
beyond (*achint*).

Perform worship (puja) at the central lotus

~ When breath automatically pauses between inhalation and exhalation, there is a gap, an interval of a split second. That pause is called a chakra in the center or central lotus between breaths. This is not an actual physical center but a subtle moment of recognition of pranic movement. Hans-breath is worshiped by the mere understanding of its nature.

Comprehend the invisible (alakh) at the lotus beyond (achint)

The "lotus beyond" is a state beyond any thoughts. *Achint* is a shapeless and formless state, and due to the absence of shape and form, it is impossible to concentrate upon it. It is also the center of imagination. By entering Achint, one who has already gone beyond mind and entered a thoughtless state will face reality that has never been seen before.

In one old Russian fairy tale a hero is given an impossible task: to go into Nowhere and find Nothing. He succeeds by simply losing his way, accepting a thoughtless state and allowing himself to wander into the unknown.

This dialog describes a similar state of "mindlessness": one needs to leave the conditioned state of mind and step beyond it to see the unseeable.

Paramhans – the Supreme Swan

गोरख उवाच

स्वामीजी! दिव्य दृष्टि किम होइवा,
किम होईबा ज्ञान विज्ञान ।
गुरु शिष्य काया कैं रहे,
किसा उतरबा पार ॥

Gorakh says:

Swami ji! How does vision become divine
(divya drishti)?

How does knowing *(gyaan)* become knowledge
(vigyaan)?

How, being in [one] body, can Guru and disciple
Go [beyond] to the other side?

श्री मच्छन्द्र उवाच

अवधू! दृष्टि ते दिव्य दृष्टि होइबा,
ज्ञान ते होय विज्ञान ।
गुरु शिष्य की एको काया,
पारचा हौ तो बहीर न जाया ॥

Shri Machhendra says:

Avadhu! From [ordinary] vision grows
divine vision.

From knowing (*gyaan*) develops
knowledge (*vigyaan*).

Guru and disciple have one body;

When [they] realize (*paarcha*) [it],
[they] don't ever leave [this body].

When Pontius Pilate asked: "What is the truth?" Jesus remained silent. Yet this text gives a precise answer: progressing from mere seeing mundane reality by developing the highest form of vision (*divya drishti*), moving towards the real knowledge of reality (*vigyaan*) and realizing it is the path to the truth.

Here "realizing" carries a much deeper meaning: it is a process of being introduced to the truth, a process of becoming a knower. At first truth is perceived as obtained knowledge; after the seeker has experienced it, lived through and with it, Gyan completes its transformation into truth and becomes true wisdom.

Breath and mind dwell in the same body: the teacher and the student both reside in the same house.

Because of pure impossibility to control and train the human mind forcefully, yogis employed breath control: they recognized its ability to influence the mental state directly and effectively.

Practitioners of higher yoga began to realize ("paarcha") – to learn, to know and consciously experience the effects of controlled breath by befriending it.

Through conscious relationship with one's own breath one can access the mind: in the beginning of this friendship breath acts as a Guru, while mind assumes the position of a disciple. Then, upon gradual awakening, mind itself becomes the teacher and breath remains an eager student, chela.

Puranas state that Atma finally becomes a teacher and mind comes to it as a student. Still, in order to witness this transformation, one has to take the path of breath.

When a true seeker rises to the level where mind strays no more, there is no return back to the state of ignorance and the ocean of Samsara will be crossed.

Upon realizing the mystery of unity of mind and breath, upon identifying itself with breath-Prana, Atma will never separate from it again; Teacher and disciple will stay in the same body together. Forever. And that's how immortality begins.

80

गोरख उवाच

स्वामीजी! कहां ते उठत श्वास उश्वास,
कहां परम हंस का वास।
कैसे मनवा निश्चल रहे,
सतगुरु होय सो पूछ्यां कहे ॥

Gorakh says:

Swami ji! Where do inhalation and exhalation
arise from?
Where is the abode of the Supreme Swan
(*param hans*)?
How does mind stay still?
You are the true Guru, kindly answer the question.

श्री मच्छन्द्र उवाच

अवधू! अरध ते ऊठत श्वास उश्वास,
ऊरधे परम हंस का बास।
सहज स्थान मनवा निश्चल रहै,
ऐसा विचार मच्छन्द्र कहै॥

Shri Machhendra says:

Avadhu! Inhalation and exhalation arise
from the middle (*ardh*).
The higher (*urdh*) is the abode
of the Supreme Swan.
Spontaneity [brings] mind to the place
where it stays still.
Thus opinion speaks out Machhendra.

༄ Prana and Apana, the Great Swan, or Paramhans, is the essence of all essences, Ishvara Himself.

Atma is Hans, and Paramatma, the Supreme Soul, is Paramhans.

Nowadays in India many people put the title of Paramhans in front of their names out of misconception or pure vanity.

In fact one can be called Hans only after becoming aware of his own Atma, or spirit. Then such a yogi will advance further in his search and will realize Paramatma, the Supreme Self. After this achievement he will be called Paramhans, as he will have met Paramatma face to face.

Flows of inhalation and exhalatin, Prana and Apana, arise in the middle ("ardh") and upper ("urdh") inner voids of the body, as well as in the void of the heart; these inner shunyas are the base for retention of energy filling all other voids of the body.

During Kriya practice of Khechari Mudra, the tongue is taken into yet another void, and this is the beginning of the state of Paramhans: mind undergoes transformation and realizes universal Prana, or the Great Swan, which resides in the Void.

Chidakash, Mehadakash etc. – these voids are extremely important for the process of realization and are described in many yogic texts.

Mental and physical access to the inner void of the body gives great powers and leads the seeker toward the Supreme Void. From purely physiological point of view, even pituitary is located inside a void, locked in the sealed chamber of a tomb-like skull.

Spontaneity [brings] mind to the place where it stays still

In the Void mind remains ever still, taken there by spontaneous realization of the Sound. Consciousness can't start developing itself because the majority of people never even try to initiate such a process.

Mind and breath long to be befriended by their carriers, but people are too busy to occupy themselves with such a task, distracted by the mundane chores. Breath and mind wait for a lifetime and finally leave the body, entering yet another shell with a hope to be finally discovered. Ordinary attention is never tuned up with mind, but a developed mind has a chance to reach its balance in the void, where it becomes absolutely still.

A dedicated practitioner enters the Void spontaneously and naturally, guided by a thread of controlled Prana and focused on the sound of Naad. There, merged with the eternal Shabd, mind regains equipoise.

--- 82 ---

गोरख उवाच

स्वामीजी! कैसे आवे कैसे जाय,
कैसे जीया रहे समाय।
कैसे तन मन सदा थिर रहे,
सतगुरु होय सो पूछ्यां कहै॥

Gorakh says:

Swami ji! How does [it] come, how does [it] go?
How does the heart remain absorbed?
How can body and mind remain
permanently stable?
You are the true Guru, kindly answer the question.

─────────────────── **83** ───────────────────

श्री मच्छन्द्र उवाच

अवधू! शून्य आवे शून्य ही जाय,
शुन हो जीया रहे समाय।
सहज शुन तन मन सदा थिर रहे,
ऐसा विचार मच्छन्द्र कहे ॥

Shri Machhendra says:

Avadhu! [Being empty] Void comes and Void goes.
Void remains absorbed in the heart.*
Spontaneously, with ease (*sahaj*),
Void always remains motionless in the body
                                          and in the mind.
Thus thought speaks out Machhendra.

ᝈ The fourth chapter of *Hatha Yoga Pradipika* speaks about the inner and outer emptiness, the need for union with the sound emanating from the Void. This fusion is the link and the path to Shunya. Absorbed and concentrated, a yogi witnesses the sound of Naad. After understanding this sound, the practitioner begins to realize the Conscious Void.

Yogis discovered the main property of Emptiness – Consciousness. By becoming conscious and aware of the Consciousness of the Void, the yogi can reach the changeless state.

────────────────

* Being absorbed by Universal Void, heart itself contains inner shunya (emptiness).

211

This particular part of the dialog is extremely important. Matsyendranath and Gorakhnath are discussing unity and duality.

Humanity remains fascinated by the concept of duality: it is said to pervade everything, while some defend universal unity.

Instead of arguing whether everything has dual or non-dual nature, a wiser thing would be to stay in the middle of it. Perhaps by recommending to take the Middle Path, Buddha meant just that: an ability to stay in the center of duality, its very point of origin – in the Void.

Here the wise ones state clearly: remain in the middle of duality. What is duality? Inhaling and exhaling manifest the ongoing duality of existence. Life happens in between these movements of Prana and Apana. Realization of life force unveils the true reality.

Gorakh himself speaks in his later poetry: "When the upper and the lower are known, there will be no more duality."

Our very bodies are the expression of duality of the egg and sperm, of past karmas of two parents, of inhalation and exhalation.

Void is the exact center of duality, the very "middle" of it. Time and Void constitute ultimate primordial Duality; they unite (this form of union can also be called Ardhanarishvara) in the transient non-duality to give birth to yet another galaxy.

Unavoidable separation follows, but the seed of Time, Bindu, starts to vibrate in the womb of the Void, giving birth to the Matter. Time impregnates the Void with a seed of creation, and this creation is dual by nature.

As a property of creation, duality never ends, but a true seeker may develop an ability to cross its borders and appraise its limits.

Such an aptitude is transformation of conscious mind into subconscious mind; a sustained subconscious state allows mind to understand higher aspects of universal dichotomy.

Only by crossing the boundaries of one state, one can truly see, appraise and remain aware of the totality of another state, which contains both of them.

--- **84** ---

गोरख उवाच

स्वामीजी! कहां बसे शक्ति कहां बसे शीव,
कहां बसे प्राण कहाँ बसे जीव।
कहां होई इनका परचा लहै,
सतगुरु होय सो पूछ्यां कहै॥

Gorakh says:

Swami ji! Where does Shakti reside? Where
does Shiva dwell?
Where does Prana live? Where does soul reside?
How can one learn and realize (*parcha*) them?
You are the true Guru, kindly answer the question.

85

श्री मच्छन्द्र उवाच

अवधू! अरध बसे शक्ति ऊरध बसे शीव,
भीतर बसे प्राण अंतरिक्ष बसे जीव ।
निरन्तर होय इनका परचा लहै,
ऐसा विचार मच्छन्द्र कहै ॥

Shri Machhendra says:

Avadhu! In the middle (*ardh*) resides Shakti;
    Above (*urdh*) dwells Shiva.
Inside lives Prana, soul resides in space
    (*antariksh*).
One should be in continuous recognition
    (*parcha*) of that.
Thus opinion gives Machhendra.

೧ Being one of the many names of Shiva, Prana is courted by its counterpart and bride Apana, who carries one of Shakti's names; both of these great forces are at play in the fields of an earthly body.

By seizing the movements of Prana and Apana and holding them still, the practitioner obtains enough realization and knowledge of these immense powers.

The seeker should remain in continuous recognition of ever-escaping Prana captured by Apana again and again; only because of Apana-Shakti Prana-Shiva remains in the body. Realization of individual soul takes place when the body's owner recognizes this play. With each exhalation and inhalation the yogi remains in the state of continuous awareness of his own jiva, which lives in the flow of Prana. Attempts to control these powers by force would be the wrong approach, but coming to friendly terms with the current of Prana and Apana in one's body would be a wise thing. Immortality starts when the yogi proves his friendship to Prana and persuades It to stay with him forever.

गोरख उवाच

स्वामीजी! कैसे बैठे कैसे चाले,
कैसे बोले कैसे मिले ।
कोण सुरत में निर्भय रहे,
सतगुरु होय सो पूछ्यां कहे ॥

Gorakh says:

Swami ji! How should one sit, how should one
walk?

How should one speak, how should one meet?

In which state of mind does one stay fearless?

You are the true Guru, kindly answer the question.

श्री मच्छन्द्र उवाच

अवधू! सुरत मुख बैठे सुरत मुख चाले,
सुरत मुख बोले सुरत मुख मिले ।
निरति सुरति में निर्भय रहें,
ऐसा विचार मच्छन्द्र कहै ॥

Shri Machhendra says:

Avadhu! Sit with awareness (surat mukh), walk
 with awareness.
Speak with awareness, meet with awareness.
Stay fearless in [the state of] absorption
 [in thoughts] (nirati) and contemplation (surati).
Thus opinion gives Machhendra.

∽ Here Guru Machhendra speaks about permanent presence in the Sound of the Void.

Consciousness ("surat") is the universal "mouth" which sings the eternal song of Naad. "Surat mukh" means to face the source, to remain with it, to be conscious of it. In the union or non-union (when conscious mind is merged with subconsiousness or in the absence of such a merger), one has to move with Naad, be absorbed in it and remain fearless. Mind spontaneously merges with the cosmic sound as the sadhak listens to Omkar while being awake and aware ("surat mukh"); he faces it by focusing and unfocusing (being attentive and becoming non-attentive). Through the constant experience of Anahat Naad one becomes permanently aware of its source. This awareness of perpetual presence in the Sound does not disrupt any daily activities: the yogi walks, talks and acts in sustained acknowledgement of Naad and at the same time with unremitting recognition of all his physical actions and surrounding world.

Extreme perception of constant presence in the Sound is a crucial part of connection with the source of this cosmic vibration – music of the Void. Without any aid of physical hearing and only through true attentiveness, the sound will register inside the practitioner's whole being.

By placing his mind between atoms and particles, the yogi realizes the Void as the carrier of all Matter and source of Its movement. That's how an ordinary mind becomes extraordinary.

गोरख उवाच

स्वामीजी! कोण है शब्द कोण है सुरति,
कोण से बंध्यो काया से निरति।
ई बंध्या मिटी कैसे रहै,
सतगुरु होय सो पूछ्यां कहै॥

Gorakh says:

Swami ji! What is a word? What is
                                    contemplation (*surati*)?
With the help of which locks [can one]
Stay absorbed [in thoughts] (*nirati*)
                                    beyond the body?
How should one live to remove barrenness
                                    (*bandhya*)?
You are the true Guru, kindly answer the question.

—————— 89 ——————

श्री मच्छन्द्र उवाच

अवधू! शब्द अनाहद सुरति सुरुचि,
निरति निरालंब लागे बंध।
कूब्ध्या मिटे सहज में रहे,
ऐसा विचार मच्छन्द्र कहे॥

Shri Machhendra says:

Avadhu! Anahad [Naad] is the word;
Contemplation (*surati*) is a good tendency.
Absorption in thoughts (*nirati*) [is achieved] by
Keeping the lock of the baseless state (*niraalamb*).
Live with spontaneity to remove barrenness.
Thus opinion gives Machhendra.

೧೨ Ordinary mind moves restlessly, sometimes clinging to a particular thought for a while. By listening to the soundless Word-Naad the seeker merges with It; his consciousness discharges the last thoughts, vivid visions and memories, completely emptying the mind of any remaining imprints.

When the yogi unites with Naad with great determination, focused only on this process, his mind enters the state of detachment, becoming "baseless" ("niraalamb").

"Niraalamb" is a thoughtless state in which spontaneity (Sahaj) of subconsciousness dominates the conscious mind, stopping the flow of "logical" constructs.

After that the "infertile woman" will not remain barren any longer.

The term "bandhya" is used here to describe unawakened Kundalini: Her sleeping energy is compared to a barren woman. This inertia prevents full activation of consciousness, sleep prolongs inability of conscious and subconscious mind to submerge into each other.

When Prana (Shiva) moves from the heart down to Muladhara chakra, it unites with the "barren woman," sleeping Kundalini-Shakti, and awakens Her.

Aroused, She becomes Prana-Shakti, reclaiming fertility in Her natural and spontaneous union with Prana-Shiva.

90

गोरख उवाच

स्वामीजी! कौण सु आसन कौण सुजान,
किहि विधि बाला धारे ध्यान।
कैसे अवगति का सुख लहे,
सतगुरु होय सो बूझ्यां कहै॥

Gorakh says:

Swami ji! What is the right posture (*aasan*);
What is the right knowing?
How should the seeker (*baala*) meditate (*dhyaan*)?
How can he delight in the joy of knowledge
                              (*avagati*)?
You are the true Guru, kindly explain.

श्री मच्छन्द्र उवाच

अवधू! संतोष सु आसन सुविचार सुज्ञान,
काया करि धरिबा ध्यान।
गुरु मुख अवगति का सुख लहै,
ऐसा विचार मच्छन्द्र कहै॥

Shri Machhendra says:

Avadhu! Contentment (*santosh*) is the right asana;
The right thought is the correct knowing.
Hold meditation (*dhyaan*) by the efforts
of physical body.
Delight in the joy of knowledge
[flowing] from Guru's mouth.
This opinion gives Machhendra.

Contentment (santosh) is the right asana

First we will define the real meaning of the word "asana" commonly used to describe yoga postures, or "yogasanas." "Asana" does not mean "posture"; it means "seat." Sitting in an asana is to be on a seat provided by the body for the spirit which inhibits it.

To "practice asanas" is to go through the process of body adjustments in the preparation of a seat for the spirit that dwells in your flesh. Finally the spirit will find a comfortable place in the body, which was prepared by holding different positions. "Holding an asana" means that the spirit finally takes the seat provided by the body.

Each and every so-called posture, described in yogic texts, is not aimed at developing the physical frame; all asanas are meant to provide a suitable environment for jiva. After becoming comfortable in the house of the body, the soul will be "in position" to start communication.

The true definition of the word "asana" is given in *Yoga Sutras*: "The pleasure of being still is asana." When a body employs stillness, then the spirit is at the peak of its comfort.

But let's make sure we are not associating stillness of the body with physical comfort. It is indeed the spirit who enjoys comfort of the stilled body, not the body itself.

Ultimate satisfaction, achieved by the practitioner when everything has been accomplished in full, comes when his ambitions have been satisfied and mind has moved beyond the fact of achievement. Everything before this achievement was just an illusion.

The state of enjoyment of a conquered goal is the state of Santosh – the supreme asana.

The right thought is the correct knowing

Here right thinking stands for focused contemplation – firm and consistent meditative state of absorbing mind. Contemplation is the process of absorption of certain knowledge or a received teaching. It is mastered by truly knowledgeable sadhaks. Without knowledge, contemplation is simply impossible.

Hold meditation (dhyaan) by the efforts of physical body

The given answer is very direct; yet again it instructs the sadhak to develop his consciousness and rise above physical constraints.

But before overcoming physical limits, these very limits should be tested and stretched in order to learn one's limitations. Then it is possible to move beyond them and to explore the unknown waiting beyond – Consciousness of the Void.

गोरख उवाच

स्वामीजी! कौण संतोष को कौण विचार,
कौण सु ध्यान काया के पार।
कैसे मनवा इनमें रहे,
सतगुरु होय सो बूझ्यां कहे॥

Gorakh says:

Swami ji! What is contentment, what is
consideration?

What is correct meditation which takes [one]
beyond [the limits of] the body?

How can one live in those [in contentment,
consideration, meditation]?

Being a true Guru, kindly explain.

93

श्री मच्छन्द्र उवाच

अवधू! निरभै संतोष अनुभै विचार,
दशो में ध्यान काया के पार।
गुरु मुख मनवा इनमें रहे,
ऐसा विचार मच्छन्द्र कहे॥

Shri Machhendra says:

Avadhu! Fearlessness (*nirbhai*) is contentment,
     understanding is consideration.
Meditation on ten [doors of the body] leads
        beyond the body.
By word of the Guru one lives in those.
Thus opinion gives Machhendra.

 "Nirbhai," or the state of fearlessness, comes when a yogi overcomes the fear of death by knowing death.

When the sadhak learns from a direct experience of Samadhi that death is just a change of the body and spirit continues to exist forever, then this great realization enters his mind permanently, bringing contentment and erasing all doubts and fears.

Meditation within the body on its ten doors will take the sadhak beyond bodily limits. It is a fact and a beautiful statement.

गोरख उवाच

स्वामीजी! कौण पांव बिन मारग,
कौण चक्षु बिन दृष्टि।
कौण कर्ण बिन श्रवण,
कौण मुखः बिन शब्द ॥

Gorakh says:

Swami ji! What is a footless path?
What is eyeless vision?
What is earless hearing?
What is a mouthless word?

श्री मच्छन्द्र उवाच

अवधू! विचार पांव बिन मारग,
निरति चक्षु बिन दृष्टि।
सुरति करण बिन श्रवण,
लौ मुख बिन शब्द॥

Shri Machhendra says:

Avadhu! Consideration is the path
                          [which requires] no feet.
[Discriminative] immersion (*nirati*) is the vision
                          without eyes.
Attention (*surati**) is hearing without ears.
Concentration is the word [which requires]
                          no mouth.

〰 All these properties belong to mind: consideration, differentiation and discrimination along with attention are not physical qualities listed in the body. Yet they "walk," "see" and "hear."

A mouthless word is mind; its mute words are the soundless whispers of thoughts.

When thoughts are ceased, then the path becomes clear.

---

* "Surati" is the union of consciousness with the unstruck sound of Anahat Naad. The absolute union of mind and cosmic sound comes with an unprecedented level of attentive yogic concentration.

―――――― **96** ――――――

गोरख उवाच

स्वामीजी! कौण धौवता कौण आचार,
कौण जाप मन तजे विकार।
कौण भाव में निरभय रहे,
सतगुरु होय सो पूछ्यां कहे॥

Gorakh says:

Swami ji! Who washes, what is [proper] conduct?
By reciting which mantra (*jaap*) does mind
                                    leave demerits?
How does one stay fearless?
You are the true Guru, kindly answer my question.

श्री मच्छन्द्र उवाच

अवधू! ध्यान धौवता विचार आचार,
अजपा जाप मन तजे विकार।
अनुभव भाव में निरभय रहै,
ऐसा विचार मच्छन्द्र कहै॥

Shri Machhendra says:

Avadhu! Meditation (*dhyaan*) washes;
    consideration is [proper] conduct.
By reciting the non-recited [mantra] (*ajapa jaap*),
    mind leaves demerits.
In the state of understanding one stays fearless.
Thus opinion gives Machhendra.

☙ Dhyan (meditation) "washes" thoughts and conduct. Through Ajapa jap (recitation of the mantra of breath – "Ham-Sah") the breather purifies his mind and gets rid of demerits. Control of breath is a step on the path to the state of fearlessness.

One abandons dismay after experiencing life in death (Samadhi). All fears are based on the dread of unavoidable death; they may be expressed in different forms, but at their root lies the fear of death, which alone terrifies an untamed mind, causing its restlessness.

By experiencing death and realizing its nature while residing in the living body, the adept accepts the fate of his body and its mortality. He will not be attached to the body any longer, as the experience of Samadhi and Gyan (the knowledge received as a result of this experience) will purify his mind and remove the fright of death forever.

For a beginner yogi, comprehension of this shloka starts with the recitation of the "mantra of breath" – Ajapa jap, which builds the awareness of one's own breath, "Ham" and "Sah." Ajapa jap is performed daily in the practice of Kriya Yoga.

This very sound comes with each taken breath in each human being: Christian, Muslim, Hindu or Jew. "Ham-Sah" does not discriminate among those whom it visits.

"The man of breath repeats the string of jap 21 600 times. Prana flows through Ida, Pingala and Sushumna day and night," says Gorakh.

Another version of "So-Ham" is "I am That," recited and chanted by sannyasis.* To describe the effectiveness of such an approach, they use a metaphor of a caterpillar who thinks of becoming a butterfly. We may note that such a transformation is absolutely natural for a caterpillar: it doesn't think of becoming a butterfly, it just becomes one in the course of evolving.

But a simple repetition of "I am That" is not going to introduce a seeker to "That" without extensive and vigorous practice of yoga.

It is conscious evolution of yogic practice that brings evolution of consciousness.

---

* Religious ascetics in Hinduism.

Prana and Apana also symbolize object and subject: "Sa" is "He" and "Ham" is "I." Practice of Ajapa jap, or "So-Ham" mantra, is an attempt to comprehend the unity between "He" and "I," between Shiva and Shakti, Jivatma and Paramatma.

गोरख उवाच

स्वामीजी! कौण स वोऊं कौण स आप,
कौण स माई कौण स बाप।
कैसे मन में दरिया रहै,
सतगुरु होय सो बूझ्यां कहै॥

Gorakh says:

Swami ji! What is Omkar? What is the self?
Who is the mother? Who is the father?
How does a river [of thoughts] flow in mind?
You are the true Guru, kindly explain.

श्री मच्छन्द्र उवाच

अवधू! शब्द बोऊं ज्योति स आप,
शुन्य स माई चेतन बाप ।
निश्चल मन में दरिया रहे,
ऐसा विचार मच्छन्द्र कहे ॥

Shri Machhendra says:

Avadhu! Word (*shabd**) is Omkar; light is the self.
Void is the mother; consciousness (*chetan*)
                                        is the father.
A river [of thoughts] flows in a still mind.
Thus opinion gives Machhendra.

Word (shabd) is Omkar

ᔪ᳁ We have already mentioned** that in Sanskrit the literal meaning of "Omkar" signifies "change of dimension, change of place."

The last sacred yogic technique performed before the final departure from the body is called Omkar Kriya. Repeated 3456 times in each chakra for the duration of one inhalation and totaling in 20736 pranayamas, Omkar Kriya signifies the yogic power of transference of the spirit.

---

* The Hindi word "shabd" can be translated into English as "word" and "sound."

** For more details, see pages 164-165.

Highly advanced yogis practice Omkar Kriya as a method of changing the dimension of the earthly plane, leaving the used physical shells of their bodies and moving on to a different address, knowing exactly their next destination.

In the process of changing dimensions of consciousness, Omkar moves mind from this mundane world to a higher plane of a different realm.

Omkar Kriya gives an exclusive possibility to a developed yogic mind to reach supreme levels of existence by transferring consciousness to its new destination with a conscious effort of a fully conscious mind.

This mystical practice allows a yogi to leave the physical plane of this carbon-based world and, by moving beyond its boundaries (and beyond carbon), to enter a place where all possible experiences and thoughts exist in their totality.

Anahat Naad, or Shabd, is the sound of "transfer" to another dimension, Omkar. This spontaneously born and omnipresent sound is independent of any physical impact. The shloka recognizes Anahat Naad as the sound of Omkar acknowledged and repeated by a yogi.

The Bible states that the initial primordial sound is the source of creation: "In the beginning there was a word, and the word was God."

Param Naad (Anahat Naad), Shabd of the Void, emanates from a formless point without a location or dimensions – Bindu, the cosmic source of the entire Creation.

Ancient rishis described Bindu, Naad and Kaal (Time) as primordial structural frame of reality.

Manifested by Bindu, the vibration of Naad becomes dense; upon reaching its condensed state, it forms the material world with the help of five elements (or "notes" of the music of Creation).

That's why everything in this world is vibratory by nature, having its roots in the vibration of Sound.

100

गोरख उवाच

स्वामीजी! कौण छै चेतन कौण छै सार,
कौण छै उत्पत्ति कौण छै काल।
कौण महिं पंच तंत जरि रहे,
सतगुरु होय सो पूछ्यां कहे॥

Gorakh says:

Swami ji! What is consciousness? What is
                                                    essence?
What is birth, what is death?
At what place do five elements continue to stay?
You are the true Guru, kindly reply to my question.

101

श्री मच्छन्द्र उवाच

अवधू! ज्योति छै चेतन निर्भय सार,
जागिवा उत्पत्ति निद्रा काल।
ज्योति में पंच तंत जरि रहै,
ऐसा विचार मच्छन्द्र कहै॥

Shri Machhendra says:

Avadhu! Light (*jyoti*) is consciousness;
                    fearlessness is the essence.
Awakening is birth, sleeping is death.
Five elements continue to stay in light.
Thus opinion gives Machhendra.

Light (jyoti) is consciousness

ᔅ The light discussed here is not a physical phenomenon –
it is the light of understanding, Gyan, dawning on the seeker.
Jyoti, effulgence and all other terms relating to light in the yogic
texts refer to the light of knowledge.

Fearlessness is the essence

By becoming awake one will begin to understand every aspect of
life and death, and with this understanding fear will disappear.
A yogi will recognize life in awakening and death in sleep, and
fear will no longer affect him: natural sleep is not to be feared
and awakening after sleep will be perceived as a natural process
(such as life after death).

Awakening is birth, sleeping is death

When conscious mind reaches subconsciousness, it enters a dreamlike state.

Awakened, mind returns back to the conscious state: such are the movements of consciousness.

Five elements continue to stay in light

Five elements dwell in the Consciousness (light) of the Void, and It binds them together in a certain proportion.

Only the supreme light of wisdom and knowledge of immense proportion can mix and paste building materials of such complexity together to create Matter so that the process of creation can continue.

गोरख उवाच

स्वामीजी! कोण बोले कोण सोवे,
कोण रूप में आपा जुग जोवे।
कोण रूप में जुग रहे,
सतगुरु होय सो बूझ्यां कहै॥

Gorakh says:

Swami ji! Who speaks, who sleeps?
In what form does the self live for ages?
In what form does [he] remain for ages?
You are the true Guru, kindly explain.

श्री मच्छन्द्र उवाच

अवधू! शब्द बोले शक्ति सोवे,
अदेख रूप में आपा जोवे।
अरूप रूप में जुग जुग रहे,
ऐसा विचार मच्छन्द्र कहे ॥

Shri Machhendra says:

Avadhu! Word speaks; Shakti sleeps.
The self lives in an invisible form.
In the form of formless [he] remains for ages.
Thus opinion gives Machhendra.

∼ Psychosomatic properties of Prana along with its cosmogony have been continuously discussed throughout this dialog. In the context of yogic practice Prana acts as a mediator between the gross body, its psyche and consciousness, uniting and binding all these aspects of individual existence.

The text gives a direct reference to Kundalini Shakti, sleeping at the base of Muladhara. The immortal spirit, or jiva, exists in the "form without form."

Individual jiva was acknowledged by ancient sages as Shiva: existing in numerous bodies, He takes them life after life, waiting for Shakti to become awoken.

It is possible that this continuous chain of rebirths is Shiva's search for Shakti. Finally She will rise and embrace Him.

By becoming aware of Shabd the yogi simultaneously recognizes Shakti, the creative force of Universal Void.

Moving further into Naad, absorbed by its sound, he discovers the Consciousness of Shakti (Void). There will be a chance that She will wake up and unite with Shiva-jiva inside the sadhak's inner void of Sushumna.

First conscious mind merges with Sound; when mind is free of any remaining thoughts, desires, constructs or concepts swept by the power of Naad, the sadhak enters the stage of Niraalamb.*

Then he becomes aware of Shakti (Void) Herself. Awareness of the Great Universal Emptiness leads to the awareness of one's own inner void – the shunya of individual body.

Kundalini Shakti is asleep in the very core of the inner individual void. With the realization of such an interconnecting phenomenon as Universal Cosmic Void and its speckle, inner emptiness and individual energy dwelling in the body, with persistent sadhana and Guru's grace, the sadhak might awake the force of his Kundalini.

Finally, Shiva and Shakti will unite and live forever, "happily ever after." But after their union the concept of Time will become different for such a seeker: his mind will perceive no more "before" and "after." For him "present" and "now" will become everlasting reality.

Transformed consciousness of the body, which underwent incredible readjustment after the union of great powers, will continue to exist in the changed concept of time forever and will remain the same through ages.

---

* For more details on Niraalamb, see page 223.

104

गोरख उवाच

स्वामीजी! कौण मुख रहणा कौण मुख ध्यान,
कौण मुख अभिरस कौण मुख पान।
कौण मुख छेदी देही रहे,
सतगुरु होय सो बूझ्यां कहै॥

Gorakh says:

Swami ji! In which mouth should one remain,
In which mouth [is] meditation (*dhyaan*)?
Which mouth does the immortal elixir
                                    [come] from?
Which mouth should one drink [it] with?
In which mouth does [the immortal spirit of]
                                    a mortal being remain?
You are the true Guru, kindly explain.

105

श्री मच्छन्द्र उवाच

अवधू! सहज मुख रहना भक्ति मुख ध्यान,
गुरु मुख अमीरस चित्त मुख पान।
आशा मुख छेदिवा देही रहे,
ऐसा विचार मच्छन्द्र कहे॥

Shri Machhendra says:

Avadhu! Remain in the mouth of spontaneity
(*sahaj*);
Dhyan [remains] in the mouth of devotion.
From the mouth of Guru [flows] the elixir of
immortality;
Drink [it] with the mouth of [your] mind (*chitt*).
By piercing the mouth of hope
[the immortal spirit in] a being remains.
This thought gives Machhendra.

The main postulate of the Naths' teaching is: Reside in Life and meditate on Death.

To experience Life in Its totality, one needs to realize what Death is. These two phenomena complement each other; they are different sides of the same coin of eternal existence. At the moment of death, Apana finally releases Prana, allowing it to leave the body forever; that is how Shiva is freed by Shakti. Life continues as long as Apana remains in the body: it is able to attract and capture pranic force, to invite Prana to the body again and again.

In a well-known Indian myth, already mentioned in reference to its symbolic connection with Khechari Mudra, gods were stirring and churning the ocean, trying to get Amrita with the help of Mount Meru.

Erected like the legendary mountain, the tongue is inserted behind the soft upper palate in Khechari Mudra and firmly held there; cerebral fluid of the brain is churned with the intense movements of head in advanced kriyas.

The sadhak literally stirs his mind, following the secret teaching: with his tongue installed in Khechari Mudra and with special head rotations, the ocean of brain is churned.

First Jivatma excretes all the poison of the outer world from the mind. Then the elixir of immortality will flow.

By piercing the mouth of hope [the immortal spirit in]
a being remains.

Line after line this shloka states: one can achieve immortality under Guru's guidance through developed consciousness while residing in the physical body.

By controlling the mouth of hope, the spirit controls all desires, and such a yogi steps beyond all kinds of attachments, sentiments and passion.

Hope needs to be recognized as an inherent property of mortals. Undying spirits and immortal beings exist beyond the notion of hope. They have no anticipations, they know no recumbence.

Faith in the words of the Teacher moves the yogi beyond any expectations. Guru's words do not grant resort, but they provide definitive information which will plant permanent inner belief in the seeker's heart.

Persistent practice, absorbed knowledge and unshakable faith will take a mortal adept beyond hope. Such a spirit may stay in the chosen body forever, overcoming physical mortality.

गोरख उवाच

स्वामीजी! कौण मुख आवे कौण मुख जाय,
कौण मुख होय काल को खाय।
कौण मुख होय जोति में रहे,
सतगुरु होय सो बूझ्यां कहे॥

Gorakh says:

Swami ji! How does one come? How does one go?
How can one devour Time?
How can one reside in light?
You are the true Guru, kindly explain.

———— **107** ————

श्री मच्छन्द्र उवाच

अवधू! सहज मुख होय आवे,
सहज मुख होय सो जाय,
निरपख होय काल कूं खाय।
निरास मुख होय ज्योति रहे,
ऐसा विचार मच्छन्द्र कहे॥

Shri Machhendra says:

Avadhu! One comes with ease (*sahaj*) and one
goes with ease.
By becoming wingless, one can devour Time.
One can reside in light by being juiceless.
Thus opinion gives Machhendra.

〰️ Guru Matsyendranath describes the climax of elaborate sadhana, when breathless state comes without effort, culminating in Keval Kumbhak. After the yogi has experienced the state of suspended animation, permanent Keval Kumbhak settles as a way of living with unforced, spontaneous breath retention.

A pot-like body holds air without inhalations or exhalations, yet the sadhak may choose to breathe while talking. However, gross speech is rarely employed by such achievers, as they are capable of mental, telepathic communication.

Dependency on oxygen gradually weakens. Eventually cell structure is permanently modified, and the physical carrier becomes indestructible, turning into a "vajra" ("diamond") body and signifying an established immortal state.

We will take a look at this shloka in detail for a better understanding of hidden hints.

One comes with ease (sahaj) and one goes with ease

"Sahaj" stands for great tolerance for challenges; all experienced emotions develop a state of natural ease of acceptance called "sahaj." The yogi who has withstood every impact of this reality with great tolerance will enter the state of Sahaj.

Being filtered through multiple experiences and tested from each and every angle, one develops patience of such a scale that his immense mental state becomes uniquely different, granting him true spontaneity and easiness in every act or thought.

In "The Sayings of Gorakh," "sahaj" is described as the saddle of consciousness:

"Make sahaj the saddle and breath – the horse,
Take the reins and whip the mind.
The rider is consciousness; make knowledge the Guru
And get rid of all deviations."

By becoming wingless, one can devour Time

"By becoming wingless," or by entering the state of breathlessness, one conquers death. Exhalations and inhalations are compared with horns of a bull or wings of a swan, Hans.

When these wings are cut, breath remains inside, unable to fly away. Such a yogi is not affected by the impact of Time and Death.

Time devours mortal bodies, but It can become food Itself for such a spirit.

Retained breath-spirit no longer has to leave the castle of the body and is not exposed to the influence of the outside world. Prolonged breathlessness, combined with full mental awareness, results in the state of Samadhi experienced prior to Keval Kumbhak.

By remaining firmly installed in control of Apana, the yogi realizes the full meaning of Prana and Life; capturing Prana with Apana, he observes their flow, fusion, play and continuity of life. As long as Apana remains with him, the sadhak will enjoy bodily life.

Spirit departs when Apana releases Prana, letting it leave the body forever. Life in the physical form is brought to close when Shiva is released by Shakti.

One can reside in light by being juiceless

The state of "niraas," or "being without the juice of life," or breath, allows one to reside in light.

All yogic texts advise to turn to Shakti, to win Her heart. And this is not an easy task even for the loyal husband. Winning the heart of Shakti will result in immense and unparalleled support from Her side and grant reward which will take the winner beyond any desire.

Poetically speaking, Apana enters her groom's house, Hriday, as a bride and meets Prana. Prana-Shiva wins the heart of Apana-Shakti and receives Her grace and propitiousness. Together they form the final and true union which will deliver immortality.

Merged, they enter Sushumna – the only place where they can remain together, breaking the cycle of duality.

In the absence of breath, intermixed Apana and Prana no longer possess their original, initial properties. We can safely state that out of their union emerges the "sixth element," which activates Kundalini energy.

This newly mixed substance can be named Ardhanarishvara – united Shiva-Shakti. Their harmonious union awakens Kundalini.

Obtained through Khechari Mudra, the elixir of immortality manifests this unity by granting eternal life to the body so it can support the supremacy of a developed mind.

The new property of united Prana and Apana, now residing in the middle channel, enables the permanent manifestation of the great Light of Moon (the bright light of Kutastha-spirit, or eternal Bindu) to remain with the practitioner.

With suspended breath, the yogi rests within his own heart, identifying with beatitude known as the bliss of Brahman (Brahmananda).

Let's summarize the process mentioned in this short shloka: the natural state of Keval Kumbhak settles; by "clipping the wings" of breath, the yogi prevails over time and death.

Conscious mind, connected with breath, becomes permanently still in the breathless condition, and subconscious mind regains consciousness. The light of his own immortal spirit and the radiance of Absolute Reality, or cognized Conscious Time, stay with the yogi forever.

गोरख उवाच

स्वामीजी! कौण है काया कौण है प्राण,
कौण पुरुष का धरिए ध्यान।
कौण स्थान मन काल सूं दुरि रहे,
सतगुरु होय सो बूझ्यां कहे॥

Gorakh says:

Swami ji! What is a body, what is
life *(praan)* [in it]?
Whom should one meditate upon?
Where does mind transcend Time?
You are the true Guru, kindly explain.

109

श्री मच्छन्द्र उवाच

अवधू! मन है काया पवन है प्राण,
परम पुरुष का धरिए ध्यान ।
सहज स्थान मन काल सू दूरि रहे,
ऐसा विचार मच्छन्द्र कहे ॥

Shri Machhendra says:

Avadhu! Mind is the body; breath (*pavan*) is
life (*praan*).
One should meditate upon the Supreme
(*param purush*).
Mind goes beyond Time (*kaal*) easily (*sahaj*).
Thus opinion gives Machhendra.

༐ Mind confirms the very fact of existence of the body; the power of breath together with the air element animate both of them.

One of the main tasks of yoga is to master the intake of Vayu by the force of breath and reinforce mind while distributing Prana to each and every cell of the body.

With successful and prolonged practice of pranayama, one develops an air body ("vayu sharir"), the pranic body, which signifies semi-immortality of the spirit and mind.

Three out of five elements of the physical body will unavoidably perish, but spirit-jiva will continue its path, merged with the elements of ether and air in Vayu Sharir.

The air element can be considered truly supreme, as it grants Atma-spirit an opportunity to travel farther and exist beyond the physical death of the body in Vayu Sharir, formed by the yogi during his lifetime by persistent practice of pranayama.

The air body will house jiva, giving an opportunity to extend the life of consciousness after the expiration of the physical body.

It is said that real practice of pranayama begins in the pranic body; when three other gross elements (fire, earth and water) exist no longer and the earthy body is gone, Vayu Sharir carries the omnipresent jiva.

Here in these earthly bodies yogis try to befriend their breath and mind by merging them into one. Once transferred into the air body, jiva becomes acutely aware of Prana and its nature, and at this moment yogic practice opens from an absolutely new angle.

The immortal substance, also called Supreme Purush, Kutastha, or Vasudev, dwells in every heart. When the seeker meets and recognizes It, this realization spontaneously takes him across the barrier of Time.

To become unreachable by Kaal (Time), one has to travel beyond the limits of physical shell by the power of mind.

Mind remains in Samadhi while body is alive and invincible to the destruction of Time. The yogi frees himself of boundaries and constraints of the physical vessel and remains beyond the grasp of death.

गोरख उवाच

स्वामीजी! कौण है कूंची कौण है ताला,
कौण है बूढ़ा कौण है बाला।
कौण स्थान मन उनमुनि रहै,
सतगुरु होय सो बूझ्यां कहै॥

Gorakh says:

Swami ji! What is a key, what is a lock?
Who is an elder, who is a child (*baala*)?
Where does mind remain transcendent (*unmuni*)?
You are the true Guru, kindly explain.

111

श्री मच्छन्द्र उवाच

अवधू! शब्द ही कूंची शब्द ही ताला,
अचेतन बूढ़ा चेतन बाला ।
ज्ञान स्थान मन उनमुनि रहे,
ऐसा विचार मच्छन्द्र कहे ॥

Shri Machhendra says:

Avadhu! Word indeed is a key, and word indeed
is a lock.
Subconsciousness is the elder; consciousness is
the child.
Mind remains transcendent in knowing.
Thus opinion gives Machhendra.

༅ The path to realization of word ("shabd") lies through the field of non-awareness of word ("nihshabd").

In the beginning of this journey, Guru graciously teaches a yogi how to become aware of the sound.

The sadhak begins to comprehend it by starting his journey from the state of Nihshabd to the recognition of Shabd, from deafness to hearing, from unawareness to the understanding of Reality and Creation.

He begins to realize the nature of subconscious and conscious mind and the process of their transformation in its totality.

Unawareness is a search for the key: one has to depart from it toward a further destination and unlock the door to awareness. The ambition to become aware of Gyan, longing for knowledge enters mind, marking the starting point of the journey towards realization. Word of the Guru is both the lock and the key for the seeker.

Being a thoughtless state as well, Nihshabd signifies stillness of mind; thoughts become immobile and undisturbed at the very source of their origin, remaining wordless and soundless.

Departing from the state of Nihshabd, the sadhak absorbs the word of the Guru, Shabd, which enables him to perceive the sacred sound of Anahat Naad.

Subconsciousness is the elder; consciousness is the child

Conscious mind is ever young and subconscious mind is old: it is their age difference that keeps us in duality.

गोरख उवाच

स्वामीजी! कौण समाधि कौण है सिद्ध,
कौण समाया कौण है रिद्ध ।
कैसे मन की भ्रांति नशाय,
सतगुरु श्याम कहो समझाय ॥

Gorakh says:

Swami ji! What is Samadhi, who is an achiever
(*siddha*)?

What is pervading [illusion], who is
a magician (*riddha*)?

How can one destroy deception of mind?

True Guru, kindly explain the twilight.

श्री मच्छन्द्र उवाच

अवधू! सुरत समाधि शब्द सु सिद्ध,
आप समाया परा है रिद्ध ।
दशों के मेटे भ्रांति नशाय,
ऐसा वचन कहे गुरु राय ॥

Shri Machhendra says:

Avadhu! Merging of mind (*surat**) is Samadhi,
                    word is a siddha.
"I" is pervading [illusion], "he" is a magician.
Deception [of mind] is destroyed by
                    erasing the ten.
In these words Guru utters his opinion.

༺ In the absence of union between conscious and subconscious mind, duality remains.

When consciousness has been developed to the level when the entire mind becomes conscious, then the adept enters the state of non-duality, gaining wholeness and unity with self, reaching beyond three gunas. By going deeper inside and remaining with one's own self, one can destroy the deception of duality.

This internal transformation can start only from within the seeker's own mind.

———————————

* The author gives the meaning of the Hindi word "surat" as the "merging of subconscious and conscious mind."

If "I" is an illusion, Maya, why does Matsyendranath refer to "he" as a magician?

The perception of "I" forms in 2% of the awakened conscious mind, while "he" consists of the remaining 98% of sleeping, unused and inaccessible subconsciousness.

The Maya of "I," or limited self, will remain until both parts can unite, merging into wholeness: then the overwhelming magic of entire consciousness will take over the illusion of limited "I."

The very act of denying the subsistence of "he" proves the fact of its existence; to wake "him" up and unite with "I" is an act of real magic.

Awareness of the Word coming from the Void gives an attentive practitioner the ability to recognize the one and only omnipresent Shabd.

This sound is the carrier of ultimate knowledge of existence of the Void and the creator of all knowledge by itself. Anahat Naad, Word of the Emptiness, is a real Siddha.

In its limitation of "I," conscious mind will never reach the state of wholeness unless it unites with "he," or subconscious self, the Siddha.

Deception of duality is destroyed when ten obstacles are erased; these five enemies and five kleshas, or mental "knots," prevent spiritual growth.

The well-known foes are greed, lust, anger, affection, false ego; the five kleshas can be listed as arrogance, ignorance, attachment, jealousy and fear of death.

गोरख उवाच

स्वामीजी! कौण है सांचा कौण से रंग,
कौण आभूषण चढ़े सुरंग।
तामें निश्चल कैसे रहै,
सतगुरु होय सो बूझ्यां कहै॥

Gorakh says:

Swami ji! What is a mold? What is color?
What is a beautifying ornament?
How should one remain still
                    upon [achieving] that?
You are the true Guru, kindly explain.

——————————————— **115** ———————————————

श्री मच्छन्द्र उवाच

अवधू! ज्ञान है सांचा प्राण सुरंग,
ज्योति आभूषण चढ़े सुरंग।
तामें निश्चल ऐसा रहे,
ऐसा विचार मच्छन्द्र कहे॥

Shri Machhendra says:

Avadhu! Knowing is a mold; Prana is
the good color.
Light is the ornament which beautifies.
Upon [becoming] still, remain changeless.
Thus opinion gives Machhendra.

ᠬᠦ World is seen in the physical light first; the light of knowledge shines when the object is focused upon.

You cannot differentiate beauty from ugliness while remaining in the darkness; both physical light and the light of understanding and knowledge will help to identify the true shape of things.

Prana, or vital breath, is called the "good color," as color represents the true element of a substance.

Poured into the mold of knowledge, vital breath transforms the mind into the splendor of True Reality.

Upon achieving stillness of mind, the yogi remains in the changeless state with the knowledge of essence of Prana.

गोरख उवाच

स्वामीजी! कौण है मन्दिर कौण है देव,
कहां बैठ करि कीजे सेव ।
कौण है पाती कैसे रहे,
सतगुरु सोई बूझ्यां कहे ॥

Gorakh says:

Swami ji! What is a temple, who is a deity (*dev*)?
Where should one stay to serve [Him]?
What is the [offering] leaf* and how does
[it] remain?
You are the true Guru, kindly explain.

---

* Traditionally, an offering in a Hindu temple is placed on a leaf.

---------- **117** ----------

श्री मच्छन्द्र उवाच

अवधू! देही मन्दिर चेतन देव,
मन सरोवर बैठ निरंतरि सेव।
प्रेम पाती उनमुन रहे,
ऐसा विचार मच्छन्द्र कहे॥

Shri Machhendra says:

Avadhu! Body is a temple; consciousness (*chetan*)
is a deity.
Serve [Him] continuously, staying
in the lake of mind.
Love is the [offering] leaf [which] remains
beyond mind (*unmun*).
Thus opinion gives Machhendra.

∾ Sometimes called unholy, the five elements of the body create an illusion of the world, or Lila. Being the building material of Maya, brick and mortar of the Void, these elements form different illusions in their endless variety of combinations.

But the human body, although consisting of "unholy" elements, becomes a shrine for the mind. The yogi worships awakened consciousness as the Supreme God, who resides in the temple of body, by remaining within it, by establishing his own self, or the real identity of "I," inside his subconscious mind. The seeker stays within and inside his own self in self-transcendence while being surrounded by the material world of elements. Such an experience is called "worship of mind."

118

गोरख उवाच

स्वामीजी! कौण है मन्दिर कौण है देव,
कौण है मूरति कौण अपार।
कौण रूप में निर्भय रहै,
सतगुरु होय सो बूझ्यां कहे॥

Gorakh says:

Swami ji! What is a temple, who is the deity
[inside it]?

What is an image (*murti**), who
is the Unfathomable?

In which form does one stay fearless?

You are the true Guru, kindly explain.

---

* Image of a deity.

श्री मच्छन्द्र उवाच

अवधू! शुन है मंदिर शब्द है देव,
ज्योति है मूरति ज्वाला अपार।
अरूप रूप में उनमुनि रहे,
ऐसा विचार मच्छन्द्र कहे॥

Shri Machhendra says:

Avadhu! Void is a temple, Word (*shabd*)
                                        is the deity.
Light is an image (*murti*), flame
                                is the Unfathomable.
Remain transcendent (*unmuni*)
                                in the formless form.
Thus opinion gives Machhendra.

गोरख उवाच

स्वामीजी! कौण है दीवा कौण प्रकाश,
कौण है बाती तेल निवास।
कैसे दीवा इन में रहे,
सतगुरु होय सो बूझ्यां कहे॥

Gorakh says:

Swami ji! What is a lamp, what is light?
Which is the oil wherein a wick resides?
How can a lamp contain them?
You are the true Guru, kindly explain.

121

श्री मच्छन्द्र उवाच

अवधू! ज्ञान हैं दीव शब्द प्रकाश,
संतोष तेल प्रेम निवास।
दुविधा मेखि अखण्डित रहे,
ऐसा विचार मच्छंद्र कहै॥

Shri Machhendra says:

Avadhu! Knowledge is a lamp, word is light.
Contentment (*santosh*) is the oil wherein
[a wick of] love resides.
[When] confusion is removed,
Remain in the wholeness [of mind] (*akhandit*).
Thus opinion gives Machhendra.

ॐ This shloka describes a body molded by the fire of yogic tapas and gives hints on attaining the state of immortality, which can be reached by a realized adept.

The lamp of knowledge burns forever, fed by the oil of satisfaction of processed Gyan and immense results brought by it.

"Santosh" is "satisfaction," the full contentment which comes after a goal has been achieved. A deep satisfaction will come after a yogi has achieved Samadhi, the highest of goals, and comprehended the secrets of everlasting life.

The depth of this satisfaction and realization of the path which led to it cause love for this path and method that resulted in the bliss of fulfilment in its totality.

Love lives in appeasement, fed by it.

In this state, yogic concentration remains uninterrupted and mind becomes steady, without any traces of past confusions.

Such a body is molded by the fire of yogic tapas, and such a realized mind has embraced the state of immortality.

गोरख उवाच

स्वामीजी! कौण बैठा कोण चल्या,
कोण किरया कोन मिल्या ।
कोण घर में निरभय रहे,
सतगुरु होय सो बूझ्यां कहें ॥

Gorakh says:

Swami ji! Who sits, who walks away?
Who acts and what is the find?
At which place does one stay fearless?
You are the true Guru, kindly explain.

123

श्री मच्छन्द्र उवाच

अवधू! बैठा धीरज चल्या विकार,
सुरति सु फिरया जिल्या सु सार।
सदा अतीत घट निर्भय रहै,
ऐसा विचार मच्छंद्र कहै॥

Shri Machhendra says:

Avadhu! Patience [of mind] sits,
                    demerit walks away.
Contemplation (*surati*) revolves [as if churned],
Essence is brought back into life [as the find].
Remain ever fearless by subtracting
                    the past (*atit ghat*).
Thus opinion gives Machhendra.

ᕟ᠊ The expression "atit ghat" gives a key to the state of fearlessness: by "subtracting" the past, one realizes the source of one's own origin, eliminating fear forever.

"Subtraction" of the past allows a yogi to discover the source of his own roots, the point of his individual emergence at the beginning of time.

Ancient mystery of one's first birth and numerous lives can be accessed, recollected and "deducted," "back forwarded" from the present moment by the very fact of recognition. Remembrance of the past is extremely important; the process of "subtraction" of the past from one's mind and life happens on conscious and subconscious levels.

The very expression "to re-member" points at re-adjustment of parts, fragments and imprints of Atma's past, which formed the foundation of the present individuality. The seeker does not "dismember" the past, but he reconstructs, recognizes and allocates the distinctive parts of it.

What is past if not a continuous chain of karmas? All past karmas will disappear in the process of recollection when the initial reason for existence, the primordial source of origin, will be understood and recognized by the sadhak.

Collective past of many incarnations, subtracted (not erased, but recognized and analyzed) from one's present life, removes fear forever: by selecting and comprehending the past, one can make a shortcut to the initial beginning, source of one's own origin.

Past is the rope which connects us with our own beginning: pull the thread or cut away its portion, and you will find yourself at the source again.

With every "death" in the breathless state or, subsequently, with every experience of Samadhi, a yogi "subtracts" his own past, becoming fearless.*

---

* Experience of "subtraction" is truly possible only in the state of Samadhi or Unmuni (beyond mind).

--- **124** ---

गोरख उवाच

स्वामीजी! कौण जोगीं कैसे रहे,
कौण भोग कैसे लहै।
सुख मैं कैसे उपजे पार,
सता में कौण बंधावे धार ॥

Gorakh says:

Swami ji! Who is a yogi and how should he live?
What is enjoyment and how to enjoy?
[Being] in happiness, how should one
                          grow beyond [it]?
What makes the stream pour into existence?

125

श्री मच्छन्द्र उवाच

अवधू! मन जोगी जो उनमुन रहै,
उपजे महारस शुब्द सु लहै।
रस ही मांही अखण्डित पार,
सतगुरु शब्द बंधावे धार॥

Shri Machhendra says:

Avadhu! Mind is the yogi that remains
                    transcendent (*unmun*).
Enjoy [and remain with] the great elixir (*maharas*)
Coming from the [Void's] Sound (*shabd*).
This elixir is indeed a great thing
                    [that] takes [you] beyond intact.
True Guru's words make the stream pour.

〰 In this shloka Guru Machhendranath instructs his disciple to remain uninterrupted in the stream of enjoyment of the great elixir by listening to the Void's Sound (Shabd). The great essence of enjoyment lies in listening, recognizing and merging with the Void. The great elixir comes as a great friend which can take one beyond.

Mind itself is a practitioner of yoga; the process will not start until it decides to learn.

Body is only a medium; it is mind who gains all experiences through the body. The main purpose of the body is to carry and deliver a developed consciousness; this task is delegated exclusively by mind.

As described in the commentary on *Shiva Sutra*,* upon taking a body, mind impregnates it with a seed of consciousness, allowing it to grow and take birth.

Wisdom brings the joy of knowledge together with the pain of it; by developing empathy and sympathy to every type of past, present and future emotions, mind obtains knowledge of all interconnected events, actions and deeds.

Not every emotion is pleasurable. When mind begins to know, understand and identify all emotions after experiencing them all, it arrives at the threshold of true wisdom.

Just like the pleasure of union eventually brings about pains of labor, eternal suffering of Samsara is tolerated with the word of the Guru which ultimately allows to overcome it.

Guru's word gives strength to withstand the burden of feelings and myriads of overwhelming emotions coming with the magnitude of such knowledge.

He who eagerly follows the word of a true Teacher develops a great tolerance.

Again and again we shall return to the perfect description of the ultimate wisdom given in this text: mind should become a disciple, while Atma acts as a Guru. Until then, the importance of the body will remain.

From early childhood we are taught to respect our birth mother; similarly, our body is the mother of consciousness and thus deserves utmost care and respect.

---

* Shailendra Sharma's yogic commentary on Shiva Sutra.

Only the mother-body can name the true father (the initial Consciousness that gave life to all of us) who remains unseen.

गोरख उवाच

स्वामीजी! कौण आत्मा आवे जाय,
कौण आत्मा शुन्य समयि ।
कौण आत्मा त्रिभुवन प्यार,*
कौण का परचा बावन बार ॥

Gorakh says:

Swami ji! Which spirit (*aatma*) comes and goes?
Which spirit merges with the Void?
Which spirit goes beyond three worlds
(*tribhuvan*)?
Whom should one realize fifty two times?

---

* Shailendra Sharma considers that due to multiple re-writing of the
original shloka from manuscript to manuscript, the Hindi word "paar"
(पार, "beyond") was misspelled as "pyaar" (प्यार, "love").

––––––––––––––––––– **127** –––––––––––––––––––

श्री मच्छन्द्र उवाच

अवधू! पवन आत्मा आवे जाय,
मन आत्मा शुन्य समाय।
ज्ञान आत्मा त्रिभुवन प्यार,
गुरु का परचा बावन बार॥

Shri Machhendra says:

Avadhu! The spirit as air (*pavan aatma*)
                              comes and goes.
The spirit as mind (*man aatma*)
                              merges with the Void.
The spirit as knowing (*gyaan aatma*)
                              goes beyond three worlds.*
Realization (*parcha*) of the Guru happens
                              fifty two times.

∾ The number 52 has several significant meanings in Yoga. There are 52 petals of chakras, 52 characters of Devanagari for Sanskrit, called "akshar" – "imperishable," and there are also 52 Bhairavas, powerful earth spirits, givers of supernatural powers, who dwell close to Shiva and Shakti. Matsyendranath states that a seeker should realize the Guru 52 times.

Guiding breath through chakras, realizing each "akshar" of each petal in each chakra unveils the identity of the inner immortal

––––––––––––––

* Hindus believe that there are seven worlds ("lok"); the word combination "three worlds" ("trilok" or "tribhuvan") refers to Earth, Sky and Space. To understand these three worlds, one should go beyond them.

spirit, the true Guru who dwells inside the body. This is "parichay" or "parcha" – the deep inner recognition, acceptance and realization of one's unperishable essence.

Dr. M. Singh's translation of this line offered another interpretation worthy of exploring. It stated, "By knowing the Guru, [a sadhak] becomes one of the fifty two heroes."

Most teachings are received on the physical plane, but some highly advanced seekers receive an astral form of initiation. A yogi who has reached a certain level in his sadhana receives an initiation from an astral teacher, who gives him a special mantra without revealing his own identity.

The Teacher who initiated a seeker into sadhana still remains a guru till the moment when an astral master appears to help a worthy practitioner advance further.

Sometimes the physical and astral guru is one and the same (as Matsyendranath). Such a guru translates the knowledge of 52 Bhairavas to his disciple.

Ideally, a teacher who is present on this earthly plane should be capable to take his disciple to the astral realm and guide him there as well as provide extended protection to the novice in this domain.

After many years, the true identity of the astral teacher will be revealed, signifying realization ("parichay") of the Guru.

From that moment, the sadhak is no longer a spiritual orphan: he acquires a new identity, becoming one of the fifty two imperishable heroes, Bhairavas.

--- **128** ---

गोरख उवाच

स्वामीजी! मन का कौण जीव,
जीव का कौण में बास।
बे श्वास का कौण आधार,
कहो आधार का कौण रूप॥

Gorakh says:

Swami ji! Who is the soul (*jiv*) of mind?
Where does this soul reside?
What is the basis of breathlessness?
Kindly say, what is the form of this basis?

--- **129** ---

श्री मच्छन्द्र उवाच

अवधू! मन का पवन जीव,
पवन का शुन्य में बास।
शुन्य का ब्रह्मा आधार है,
ब्रह्मा का अचित रूप॥

Shri Machhendra says:

Avadhu! Air (*pavan*) is the soul (*jiv*) of mind.
Air lives in the Void.*
The base of the Void is Brahm.
The form of Brahm is inconceivable (*achit*).

〜 The life of mind depends on vital air and breath; breath itself depends on the consciousness of mind, they complement and support each other. That's why learning and understanding of breath will open the deep mystery of mind. Breath is the very essence of mind.

The all-sustaining Prana pervades the Void and every element born out of Emptiness; all carriers of Matter and all carriers of consciousness are nurtured by the vitality of its force.

The form of Brahm is inconceivable (achit)

A fully conscious mind (where the conscious and subconscious parts are united) is called "Brahm" (not "Brahma").

---

* Air ("pavan") in the Void is the breathless state.

The form of full consciousness is inconceivable and unthinkable because a yogi can unite with it only by experiencing such a state in all totality. Then the full consciousness gives him his real identity, super-identity.

Try to imagine how fully awakened mind will operate: by merging with the new identity of your own mind in its totality, you will become omnipotent and present everywhere at the same time. Such a form of advanced consciousness could not be comprehended by undeveloped and limited minds.

Guru Matsyendranath

YOGIC COMMENTARY by SHAILENDRA SHARMA

गोरख उवाच

स्वामीजी !कौण चक्र शिर के कंध,
कौण चक्र अगोचर बंध ।
कौण चक्र में हंस निरोधे,
कौण चक्र में मन परमोधे ।
कौण चक्र में काल है सबाधि,
कौण चक्र में लगे समाधि ॥

Gorakh says:

Swami ji! Which chakra shoulders [supports]
                                    the body?
In which chakra [should] the unseen bandh
                (*agochar bandh*) [be applied]?
In which chakra [can] the swan be controlled?
In which chakra are mind and soul (*man*)
                                    delighted?
In which chakra does Time (*kaal*) achieved?
In which chakra can Samadhi be attained?

—————— **131-132** ——————

श्री मच्छन्द्र उवाच

अवधू! मूल चक्र थिरके कंध,
गुगा चक्र अगोचर बंध।
मणि चक्र में हंस निरोधे,
अनाहद चक्र में मन परमौधे॥

मिशुद्ध चक्र में काल समाधि,
चन्द्र चक्र में लगे सबाधि।
ए षट् चक्र का जाणे भेव,
सो आपहि करता, आपहि देव॥

Shri Machhendra says:

Avadhu! Mula chakra shoulders [supports]
                                    the body.
[Apply] the unseen bandh in Guda chakra.
Control the swan in Mani chakra.
In Anahata chakra mind and soul (*man*) are
                                    delighted.
In Vishuddha chakra Time [achieves] Samadhi.
In Chandra chakra Samadhi is achieved
                    [and becomes part of knowing].
If you know the mystery of these six chakras,
You are yourself the maker (*karta*),
You are yourself the God (*dev*).

〰 The true goal of immortality can be outlined in the
following words:

To create unlimited future for the spirit residing in the body, understanding of the importance of mind development has to be reached first; then the house of the spirit has to be fortified.

All yogic treatises list the most important tools of yogic art in the quest for immortality.

Body has to be vigorously prepared to host the spirit for eternity with the power of seven crucial bandhs and mudras: Mahamudra, Mahavedh, Mahabandh, Mulabandh, Uddiyan Bandh, Jalandhar Bandh and Khechari Mudra.

The immortal giver of Kriya Yoga, Babaji Maharaj, shared this mystical knowledge with modern-day yogis, so that hints on immortality, yet waiting to be discovered through dedicated and utterly artistic practice of Kriya, could be recognized in these mudras.

It this shloka Guru Matsyendranath describes results achieved by mastery over the body, chakra by chakra, starting from Mula center, the basis of bodily existence. Reading carefully, one can recognize Siddhasana and Mahamudra as practiced in Kriya Yoga.

Let's take a look: Agochar Bandh, or Mulabandh, takes place in Mula; Mani chakra is under control; fire moves up from the Nabhi center; Prana in union with Apana rides on the back of the awakened serpent energy through the heart, throat and head centers; and the accomplished mastery of activation of these chakras grant life in eternity.

Muladhara, or Mula, represents the earth element. Only after the element of our planet is recognized and realized by a yogi in his own earthly body, immortality can be achieved.

Matsyendranath instructs: "Sit on the shoulders of Muladhara (the earth element) and hold Agochar Bandh (the unseen bandh) there." It actually means "apply Mulabandh in Muladhara."

This bandh can't be seen, as even the most accomplished yogis can't demonstrate it due to its location.

We already know that the initial development of embryo starts from Mula, Guda and Nabhi centers simultaneously.

These life-receiving nodes can be reactivated again, and the mechanism of creation will start to rejuvenate and sustain the adept's body anew.

If a yogi is able to control these centers, he reverses the ageing process, defeats time and old age, stepping into eternity.

Skillful control of Mula and Guda (anus) centers also redirects the current of sexual energy; tamed sexual impulses and the reversal of its outward flow can grant a brahmachari* a possibility to prolong his life. A sadhak directs it inward and absorbs its creative essence.

Sexual impulse (not the sexual organs and centers) ignites the basic feeling of sexual desire; it grows from one's survival instinct: to save the genetic code by carrying it forward in time. Procreation program, triggered by the sexual instinct, is the only way to leave one's individual genetic trace. That's why the fear of death is the basis of sexual desire.

If achieved, immortality cures this fear forever, sexual urges are ceased, and, transformed by the tapas, the essence of DNA of one's body sustains its longevity.

---

* An adept who practices brahmacharya – celibacy.

Control the swan in Mani chakra

Manipura chakra controls Swan-breath. Swan (Hans) flies in and out of the body in the seed mantra of the exhaled breath in the sound of "Ham," and the inhalation brings the sound of "Sah."

Via Nabhi center, and specifically through bank naal, the intake and distribution of life force is reined.

Paramhans is the Universal Soul, or Paramatma, Ishvara. He is the Swan of the swans, Jiva of all jivas, also known under the name of "God" for lack of better terms.

Breath can be controlled with recognition of Prana and its taming. This process starts with realization of jiva's true nature and is followed by liberation from all limitations.

Nabhi Kriya, performed at the navel center, is employed as a powerful tool for reactivation of life force. Let's take a step back to remind ourselves why yoga stresses the importance of prolonged life in the physical body.

Longevity of body is achieved through successful activation of bank naal with Nabhi Kriya. It switches on the mechanism of body rejuvenation.

The goal of achieving and sustaining everlasting life in one's body is to have enough time to realize the Time. Controlled Nabhi prolongs life so that a sadhak can change his perception of Time flow by controlling Vishuddha and observe it objectively, gaining new knowledge and experience.

Anahata is the center of domain of the unstruck sound of Anahat Naad. It dwells all around us, born in the great cosmic Emptiness – Void.

Mind and soul experience utmost pleasure listening to the word of the Void (Naad) and recognizing it in the heart. The yogi reaches ultimate satisfaction and happiness upon receiving this Word.

Vishuddha is a crucial junction for the flow of vital energy from the brain.

Physiologically, the throat center consolidates myriads of nerves and nadis, running down to the other parts and organs of the body, connecting "upper" with "lower." Vital air and food are supplied through this center; it directly affects Hriday, which refines and collects pranic energy received via Vishuddha.

Control of this center in Kriya is achieved with particular head movements, through physicality, but effects lead far beyond.

In Vishuddha chakra Time [achieves] Samadhi

Unless you stop the flow of time, it cannot be fully realized as it moves continuously. At least it appears moving to our mind, as mind itself remains in constant rotation. To stop time is to suspend your own sense of time perceived by the brain, by bringing mind and senses into the state of suspended animation. When mind stops, then it observes time objectively.

As long as a fish continues to live in the water, it will never see it. To form perception of water, the fish has to get out of the ocean. Only then it will understand what water is.

The same example applies to us. Living inside Time, we never perceive it in full: our cognition of time is narrow and limited. Control of Vishuddha brings the body in the state of suspended animation, and then Time does not affect it any longer.

In *Chandra* (Agya) chakra Samadhi of the mind begins. Synonymous with mind, Chandra signifies real awareness. Controlled Vishuddha brings the body in suspended animation. After mind has experienced and understood this state, the yogi becomes "knowing," or realized.

In Chandra chakra the knowledge of Samadhi becomes part of knowing. Different from knowledge, knowing is a state of experienced Truth.

> *If you know the mystery of these six chakras,*
> *You are yourself the maker (karta),*
> *You are yourself the God (dev)*

The main objective of yoga is to establish connectivity with Mother Earth, the cradle of powerful energy, which holds the key to the door leading to the Supreme Mind.

All yoga and tantra texts describe this force as an inert serpent resting in three and a half coils in Muladhara chakra. The bearer of the earth element, Mula houses this vital energy, which guards the gates to everlasting life in the state of supreme consciousness.

The element of earth is real Shakti that nurtures and protects the power of Kundalini.

When a yogi connects with the energy of Earth, it will pass through his earthly body, linking and merging all elements responsible for "compilation and assemblage" of his present physical shell.

The entire text of *Gorakh Bodh* carries fragmented description of different phases of this great journey, during which Kundalini, "the coiled one," springs up and rises, piercing chakra by chakra, element by element, reaching the spirit-jiva and uniting it with the Higher Mind.

Let's follow this mystical path: Prana Shakti comes down from Hriday into Muladhara, connects with its earth element and awakens Kundalini.

As a result of certain contractions and controlled breathing, the coiled energy is forced to leave its seat, to straighten and pierce Sushumna, spinning and whirling up from Mula to Nabhi.

Ascending, it crosses Swadhisthana chakra and merges with its tattva, the water element. Then it pierces Manipura and merges with the fire element, the basis of life.

Climbing higher, Kundalini arrives at Anahata, the embodiment of the air element that evolved from the ether.

From there it rises to Vishuddha, or Bharatisthana, located above Anahata at the bottom of the throat ("kantha mula"), the embodiment of the sky element.

In Agya chakra (also called "Param Kula" and "Mukta Triveni" due to its separation in Bhrumadhya into three channels – Ida, Pingala and Sushumna) the rising energy detects only the subtle tattva of mind. Now the "gross" tattvas (elements), strung on the axis of the rising energy, are left behind.

Then Kundalini reaches Param Shiva in Sahasrara chakra. The yogi attains his true home; he is free, omnipotent and omnipresent.

Passing Sahasrara, where Param Shiva is manifested as Great Ether ("paramakash rupa") the energy exits beyond all centers and chakras of the physical body, entering the aspect of Absolute. At this moment mind reaches a state beyond consciousness – Unmuni.

Having passed through the physical body, the supremacy of the earth energy transforms it into a "diamond body"; mind opens up and becomes Supreme.

पवन पवना साधंते योगी,
जरा पलटे काया ह्वा निरोगी।
साधो अवधू योग कला,
निश्चय साधे होये भला॥

Yogis practice [the art of] breathing (*pavan*)
and vital air (*pavana*),
Reverse old age and [make] a body
not stained by disease.
Avadhu! Practice the art of yoga, practice
with full determination;
It will do you good.

〜 Only an exceptional yogi, whose Kundalini energy has risen, piercing and activating all six chakras, possesses real knowledge and accomplishes the goal of yoga.

As a result of dedicated practice, energy ascends along Shankhini nadi (Sushumna) through the fluid of the spinal cord, refurbishing and igniting all chakras one by one, finally reaching "the crown" – Sahasrara.

Gained control of Mula and Vayu, combined with the knowledge of *nilata* in *lalata*,* will enable the practitioner to enter his own consciousness.

---

* In Kriya Yoga, "nilata in lalata" indicates the passage of the tongue in Khechari Mudra behind the upper palate, past inner nasal cavities into the space from where Kutastha emerges.

"Lalata" means "forehead"; "nilata" is "going inside," "entering forbidden territory out of reach"; the tongue does not stimulate any center physically, but it triggers the appearance of the immortal spirit.

Powerful activation of all six chakras inside the median channel will lead to the experience of Samadhi. Such a yogi becomes a master of Sushumna; he is the cause of his own existence or self-annihilation.

Behind the doors of Samadhi opened with this mystical knowledge, the yogi will find the greatest of pleasures.

Jai Guru Matsyendranath!

I bow down to the lotus feet of the greatest of the Gurus of Yoga and direct disciple of Adinath.

May His grace be upon us, yogis.

We hope to receive His blessing.

Jai Gorakhnath, Jai Machhendra Guru ki!

Sources and References

Several original works of the Nath Siddhas have been subjected to a relatively modest number of detailed studies in the West, although widely referred to and commented upon by the researchers of Indian religious cults, yoga and alchemy.

The following sources were used in the present publication for the in-depth analysis of original texts and refinement of the English translation.

"Gorakhnath and Medieval Hindu Mysticism"

The first comprehensive English interpretation of *Gorakh Bodh* was pioneered by Dr. Mohan Singh in his work "Gorakhnath and Medieval Hindu Mysticism" (Lahore: Oriental College 1937). The English translation, widely available on the internet, has no reference to Mr. Singh's authorship, but undeniably belongs to him in light of the absence of other known publications in the English language.

A copy of undated manuscript with some missing pages, written in old Hindi or, rather, in pidgin Sanskrit and mix of Paishachi, Apabhramsa and Desi languages under the title "Gorakh Bodh. Swami Sevak Sambad" was found by Mr. Singh in the Punjab University Library of Lahore.

Professor Singh named this mixture of dialects "Hindwi." He also observed that this type of language can be called "Khari Boli" or "Sant Bhasha" and that it bears a clear linguistic imprint of Kshatriyas, Rajputs, Ahirs and Gujjars of the lower classes.

He obtained another manuscript (a copy of the same text) from the State Library of Jodhpur: this text had several more lines, connected with six chakras and nerve centers. The third manuscript, available at Jain Mandir of Patti, was also studied by Mr. Singh during his research.

"Shree Gorakh Bodh Vani Sangrah"

The present publication of "The Twilight Language of Gorakh Bodh" cites the original Hindi shlokas from the third edition of "Shree Gorakh Bodh Vani Sangrah" ("Shree Gorakh Bodh. Collection of Sayings") by Swami Ramprakash Maharaj Agrawat. This book was published by Phoolchand Bookseller, Purani Mandi Ajmer. The editor and commentator of this text states that he received the original manuscript in the summer of 1783, but the year of the publishing is unknown. The book contains several texts, including dialogs between Gorakhnath and Dattatreya, Gorakhnath and Ganesh, and bhajans.

Published under the subtitle "Gorakh Bodh Bhajan Mala," the dialog between Matsyendranath and Gorakhnath has yet another title – "Resolution of Student's Doubts by the Teacher" ("Shree Guru Shishya Shanka Samadhan").

It is possible that the text had been rewritten numerous times before Swami Agarwat obtained it in 1783. In the introduction he also mentions the name of the person who recorded the text – Biramdas ji, the grandson and disciple of Ramjidas ji Maharaj and also a disciple of Sri Tulsidas ji. In all likelihood, it refers to the famous poet Tulsidas.

Gorakh Bani

Several quoted stanzas from *Gorakh Bani* ("The Sayings of Gorakh") are given in English translation by Mr. Shukdev Singh and Gordan Djurdjevic ("Masters of Magical Powers: The Nath Siddhas in the Light of Esoterical Notions" (University of British Colombia, 2005).

Some shlokas of *Gorakh Bodh*, translated by Mr. Singh in his book "Gorakhnath and Medieval Hindu Mysticism," are absent from the original Hindi text in "Shree Gorakh Bodh Vani Sangrah."

However, from the yogic point of view, the author of the present publication Shri Shailendra Sharma considers these stanzas to be authentic, therefore, they were commented upon.

Marked as "MSP" (Mohan Singh Publication), these lines are placed in accordance with their logical sequence in "The Twilight Language of Gorakh Bodh."

Katia Mossin

Acknowledgements

Concept and interviews: *Ilya Khanykov, Katia Mossin*
Literary editing: *Katia Mossin*
Technical editing: *Maria Pistunova*
Hindi translation: *Shailendra Sharma, Ella Simorova*
Cover design, markup and illustrations: *Farida Idiyatullina*
Proofreading: *Ella Simorova, Aditya Naredi, Prachi Jawlekar, Hitesh Borad, Sergey Nazarov*
Special thanks to *Anju Kalra, Bhushan Jawlekar*

Other Publications

In the early 90s, over a period of 14 months, yogi Shailendra Sharma produced several extraordinary masterpieces of literature. The content of these books transcends the basic categories of religion, spirituality, New Age and philosophy. It is a collection of profound experiences manifested through an intense practice of yoga leading to unfathomable states of self-realization and original thought. For over 28 years, truth seekers from around the world have visited him to hear his practical wisdom and have received answers to some of life's biggest questions.

Yogeśvarī Śrīmadbhagavadgītā:
A Yogic Commentary

Śrīmadbhagavadgītā, simply known as Gita, is one of the primary sources of spiritual knowledge in the Indian tradition. Many commentaries on Gita were available, but there was not a single commentary written by a yogi. This inspired Shailendra Sharma to write such a work revealing the hidden secrets of life: Time Itself speaks from the pages of Gita, being the Supreme God. The author has explained the knowledge that has come down via his lineage of Gurus as well as realized through his own ardent practice of yoga.

Yoga Darśan:
A Yogic Commentary

Patanjali's Yoga Sūtras, also known as Yoga Darśan, is a fundamental text of the yogic tradition, one of the six traditional schools of Indian philosophical thought. Four short chapters consisting of 196 sutras concentrate the quintessence of yogic wisdom. Despite the brevity, it is the most poetic and inspirational work among the sacred texts on yoga. Only a practicing yogi can fully comprehend the meaning of the text after the realization of the states described in the book, and Shailendra Sharma does it brilliantly. This book is an English translation of the original Hindi commentary of *Yoga Sūtras*.

Śiva Sūtra:
A Yogic Commentary

About 250 years ago, a Kashmiri Brahmin named Vasugupta was directed in a dream by Lord Shiva Himself to find a huge rock in a cave on the Shankara Hill. He was told that he would receive the spiritual knowledge bestowed by Shiva Himself. He was directed to absorb it and spread it in the society. The very next day 77 sutras carved on a rock were discovered. These sutras are short but multidimensional and are capacious aphorisms about the exact methods of realization. Shailendra Sharma gives commentaries on this sacred text, being guided by the vision found after long years of persistent yogic practice.

Hatha Yoga Pradipika of Swatmarama:
A Manual of Kriya Yoga

One of the most mysterious ancient yogic texts, *Hatha Yoga Pradipika* describes in great details every step on the path to self-realization. This unique edition pioneers remarkable commentaries by a realized yogi. Expositions by Shailendra Sharma, the Fifth Guru of Babaji Maharaj parampara, explain in precise details sequences of Kriya Yoga practice as per traditional teachings of this lineage.

Some Flowers And Some Thorns

Collection of aphorisms and thoughts, an assortment of flowers and thorns from the garden of life – wisdom that only a yogi can impart.

The Wayfarer

Our spirit is a traveler. While braving the path of life, the author is sharing his observations and experiences with other wayfarers in the form of inspirational poems.

At The Right Hand of God:
Selected Darshans

A collection of Shailendra Sharma's daily conversations with his disciples and visitors displays a variety of topics arising from a wild array of questions posed to him in the last twenty years. Describing powerful Kriya Yoga techniques, explaining ways to discover your own immortal substance, redefining the very perception of God, Time, and Creation from a yogic point of view, this book is for the seekers of truth.

Books are available on
www.gurujibooks.com or *www.amazon.com*

For more information about the author visit
www.shailendrasharma.com

Printed in Great Britain
by Amazon

26341886R00178